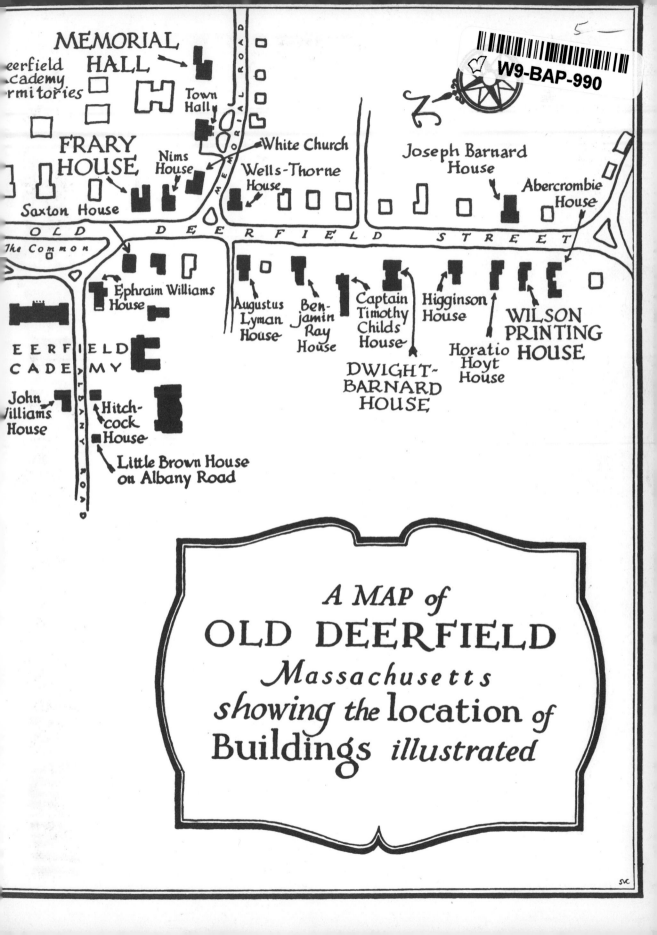

A MAP of
OLD DEERFIELD
Massachusetts
showing the location of
Buildings illustrated

HISTORIC DEERFIELD

FRARY HOUSE

HISTORIC DEERFIELD:

HOUSES AND INTERIORS

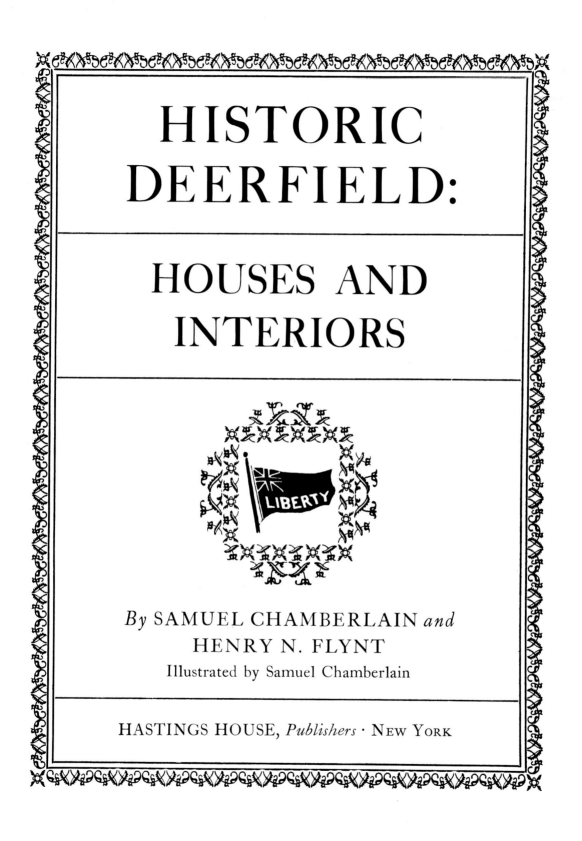

By SAMUEL CHAMBERLAIN *and*
HENRY N. FLYNT
Illustrated by Samuel Chamberlain

HASTINGS HOUSE, *Publishers* · New York

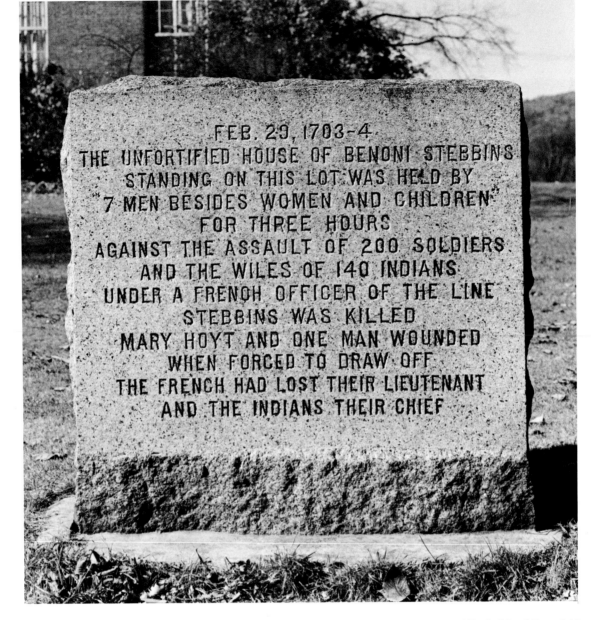

The Spirit of Deerfield

REVISED AND ENLARGED EDITION OF "FRONTIER OF FREEDOM"
COPYRIGHT © 1965, 1957 & 1952 BY HASTINGS HOUSE PUBLISHERS, INC.
PRINTED IN THE UNITED STATES OF AMERICA
LIBRARY OF CONGRESS NO.: 65-17610

PROLOGUE

Our young and powerful nation finds itself in this third quarter of the twentieth century engaged in an ideological conflict in many parts of the world. A constant challenge is being hurled at us. This challenge comes from sundry sources and by various means. It may come from violent Communist invectives or from the too hospitable forum of the United Nations Assembly. It may come from incendiary editorials or from insidious posters plastered on city and village walls throughout Europe, portraying the United States as a monstrous octopus with dollar signs for eyes. Most consistently it comes over the air waves or the foreign press, a repetitious slander employing the same stock phrases . . . . "Warmonger," "Imperialist," "Capitalistic Tool of Wall Street" . . . . with the monotony of a tom-tom.

To the native American, and to the stranger who lives in our midst, the charges are preposterous, so completely far-fetched that they seem not to call for an answer; but our ideological opponents have availed themselves of an old technique . . . . repeat a false accusation often enough and it gains acceptance as fact. Two decades ago our most obvious answer was a mighty one—the Marshall Plan, the greatest single act of generosity in history.

Other replies to the vilification of the Communists do not need to be couched in calumny or hollow phrases. They can even be expressed pleasantly. Visual truth can speak louder than words in contradicting propaganda. A graphic picture of one of a hundred phases of American life—a state university, a model factory, a western farm, a New England village—can be the most eloquent response to the strident falsehoods poisoning the air today. We have chosen the symbol of a specific village street. Among many others, it demonstrates the calm strength of America today. Its story is one of daring and courage, of bloodshed and tragedy, of fiery patriotism, cooperative effort, friendliness and love of life. Even though this village heard the piercing screams of the Indians two and a half centuries ago, its people met the challenge as we are meeting it in far-flung parts of the world today with the lives of brave men and women.

Time has healed the wounds which afflicted this martyred outpost. After decades of repose it stands today verdant, serene and venerable, yet very much alive as a community. American taste and culture, American eagerness for learning and respect for the past, all these are summed up in this tranquil community. Such a village street didn't happen easily. It was fired in a crucible of suffering and boundless courage. Brave people made the beautiful thoroughfare whose image is printed at the top of this page, "The Street" of Old Deerfield, Massachusetts.

A flag flies from a pine pole at one significant point along "The Street." It is not the flag we are accustomed to see, but the Taunton flag, a British red ensign with the word "LIBERTY" sewn in white across the lower part of the field. Here in July, 1774, the local "Sons of Liberty" erected the Liberty Pole in front of David Field's store, the rallying point for the village patriots. Here the Taunton flag still flies, as a symbol of our country's highest ideal, the principle of freedom.

FRONTIER OF FREEDOM

PART I

If the aspirations, ideals and struggles of the American people could be summed up in one word, that word is emblazoned boldly on the Taunton flag pictured on the opposite page. Love of liberty has been the keystone of our existence, from the moment the first Pilgrims set forth for the New World. Liberty means so much to us that the word itself seems inviolate. Apply it to bonds, bells or ships, it still retains its dignity, its grip on the hearts of men. The pursuit of liberty and a better life has ever been the motivating force of the American, whether he be farmer, fisherman, merchant, craftsman or fur-trapper. It has dictated the growth of his family, his house, his village. It explains his Christianity, his persistence, his ingenuity and eagerness to seek out new and uncultivated fields. It has led him to suffering and hardship and cruel death. But the magnetic force of liberty never falters. A new generation is ever ready to carry the torch.

The individual occupies a wondrous place in this country. His freedom, his rights, his dignity form the bedrock foundation of our democratic way of life. Integrated into a disciplined society, but still retaining his right to go as far as his honest enterprise will take him, the free individual is our answer to Marxism, to the siren song of collectivism, to the stifled churches and carefully concealed People's Paradises behind the Iron Curtain.

Democracy has its flaws, one of the most apparent being the abuse of its liberties by its own beneficiaries. We have achieved no Utopia in this Republic. We have no cause for smugness, but we can rejoice that the ideal of liberty burns as vividly as ever, and that the freedom which our ancestors achieved at such a heavy price has been preserved as our inheritance.

If so much can be expressed in a single word, is it not possible to sum up the strength of this Republic, its vigor and idealism and enterprise, in a single American community? This book is based on the thesis that this is possible, and that captioned photographs can tell the story with eloquence and beauty. To support this contention, we are turning not to a typical American village, but to an extraordinary one. It is extraordinary, not only for its present tranquil charm, but for its courageous, blood-stained place in American history. The name of this village is Old Deerfield, Massachusetts. In its day it was the white man's farthest outpost in the wilderness. Today it rests quietly on its slight plateau in the Connecticut Valley, surrounded by rich fields of tobacco and corn, and hemmed in by wooded hills. A kind Providence has placed it a few hundred yards off the main highway, thus preserving its venerable street from the roadside encroachments which all too often disfigure the landscape today. Without making a conscious effort, it stands as a living monument, and an almost unblemished one, to the early Americans and their reassuringly civilized way of life. From the hazardous seventeenth century until the present, this mile-long village street has clung to its past, keeping up its ancient houses and cherishing the fruits of freedom so dearly bought by its pioneer settlers. But it is not a sleepy village, subsisting on its laurels alone. It is a vigorous, alert community, devoting its energies particularly to education. Something else sets it apart. Many of its handsomely furnished houses are permanently open to the public. Thus it has several of the virtues of other assembled or restored communities in this country, while retaining its village life unchanged. Its fields and meadows at each end of the village are still farmed by local men, proud of their life and what the community stands for in today's American scene.

Deerfield is by no means the only town which could serve as a symbol of the American story. Other significant names come to mind at once— Plymouth, Lexington, Williamsburg, Yorktown, Valley Forge, Gettysburg. Why does this particular village seem so well fitted for the honor? One reason is its remarkable state of preservation. Another is that Deerfield, from its inception in the 1660's up to the present time, has *lived* the American drama without interruption. Its citizens have been normal, courageous, God-fearing people, not necessarily heroes or paragons of virtue. But their story has been an epic in our history. George Sheldon, the venerable historian of Deerfield, needed two plump volumes to do justice to his theme. It is with fitting apologies that the Deerfield story has been condensed within these few pages.

If his Majesty's surveyors in the Massachusetts Bay Colony had been in closer contact with the members of the General Court, the story of Deerfield might have been different. In fact, it might not have existed at all. It did not take form in the same way as did other seventeenth-century communities. It began as an advance outpost in the wilderness, an isolated grant of land surrounded by Indians who were friendly at first but were urged on by other tribes to become hostile. This ominous beginning was due to a land dispute between what are now two of Boston's most respected suburbs, Dedham and Natick. The difficulty arose when the philanthropic Lady Mary Armeyne, granddaughter of the Earl of Shrewsbury, established a fund of twenty pounds per annum for missionary purposes in New England. The General Court awarded the prize to John Eliot and gave him a generous tract of land for his Christian Indian settlement at Natick. Regrettably enough, the land proved to belong to Dedham, and not to Natick, a situation which led to twelve years of bickering between the two towns. In 1663 the General Court decided that a recompense was due, and judged "meete to graunt Dedham eight thousand acres of land in any convenient place or places not exceeding two where it cann be found free from former graunts."

The more adventurous citizens of Dedham were soon foraging in the interior wilderness in search of fertile acres yet unclaimed. When they came upon this broad, loam-laden tract in the Connecticut River Valley, they sought no further. The English had already settled the southern stretches of the valley. From New Haven northward through Wethersfield, Hart-

The Ashley House

ford, Windsor, Springfield and Northampton, their farms stretched out thinner and thinner. Farther north the land became an unbroken wilderness all the way to Montreal. John Pynchon, son of one of the founders of Springfield, and the most active trader in the region, was commissioned to buy the title to 8,000 acres north of Hadley from the Pocumtuck Indians. This tribe had once been proud and powerful, maintaining its supremacy until the middle of the seventeenth century when a fierce war broke out between it and the marauding Mohawks. After that only a sad fragment of the Pocumtucks remained. They were probably weary and in need of the white man's wampum. At all events, the transaction was closed with comparative ease in 1667. The price paid was considered very high—fourpence per acre. Deeds for a part of this historic purchase are still on exhibition in the village.

There was a lull of more than three years before the first enterprising settler arrived on the scene in the spring of 1669. This was Samuel Hinsdell of Hadley. He brought his thriving family with him and they lost no time in breaking ground on the inviting, mile-long plateau. He was soon followed by Samson Frary of Hatfield. Things moved rapidly after that. The struggle against nature and hostile man had begun. By 1673 twenty families had arrived. They helped each other build houses and plant fields. Their names have a familiar ring in the Deerfield of today . . . . Allen, Barnard, Clesson, Field, Frary, Hawks, Hinsdell, Nims, Smead, Stebbins, Tuffts, Sheldon, Wells. By the spring of 1673 the community had laid out its village street, and apportioned its house lots essentially as they remain today. The first white child native to the settlement was born to the Hinsdells and bedecked with the name Mehuman.

Bloody Brook Tavern

In May of that year the citizens petitioned to establish an independent town, a request which the General Court granted "provided that an able & orthodox minister within three years be settled among them." The eager townspeople lost no time. Before the year was out the young Reverend Samuel Mather, one of the family of famous clerics in the eastern part of New England, arrived and served as the first minister of Pocumtuck. The wheels of progress marched on and in other directions. In September of the following year Moses Crafts of Roxbury was licensed to open an ordinary in the village and to "sell wines & strong liquors for one year, provided he keep good order in his house." The name of Deerfield first began to creep into official papers in 1674. Its scattered population had reached the impressive figure of 125. The frontier farmers were reaping good wheat harvests, but apprehension grew. Hemmed in between the hills, the settlers were constantly aware of the threat of Indian raids. Citizens carried guns everywhere, even in church. The atmosphere was tense, yet it looked for a time as though the little outpost would hold its own. After all, up to that time not a single Englishman in the Connecticut Valley had lost his life in armed conflict with the Indians.

Then came the fateful month of September, 1675, on the first day of which Deerfield was attacked by a band of sixty Pocumtucks. They hid in the woods, waiting stealthily for a chance to catch the villagers off guard. They were foiled in this attempt when James Eggleston, a soldier, stumbled in their midst while hunting for his horse. He was killed on the spot, but the sound of the gun warned the settlers who raced to the stockades. These fortifications, each manned by twelve citizens, proved too strong for the Indians. They retreated, after burning outlying buildings and crops. A second attack fell on the 12th of September and was also repulsed, but on the 18th disaster overtook the white men. To supply the encampment at Hadley, where food was running low, Major Pynchon ordered part of the available wheat to be shipped there by ox-cart. Captain Thomas Lothrop of Beverly and his "choice company of young men, the very flower of the County of Essex," were ordered to accompany the convoy. For two miles the procession plodded through the south meadows until they came to a sluggish brook almost concealed by wild grape vines. The fragrant temptation was too much. The thirsty teamsters and their convoy stopped to taste the ripe grapes. The fateful pause was a signal for attack. A shrieking horde of Nipmucks, Wampanoags and Pocumtucks swarmed upon them from the thicket and achieved an almost total massacre. Only a handful of brave men survived.

Completely outnumbered by more than seven hundred of King Philip's Indian warriors, the white men were almost obliterated. Seventeen Deerfield men had voluntarily placed themselves under Lothrop's command that day. Their names are also familiar today—Allen, Barnard, Barsham, Carter, Gillet, Hinsdell, Plympton, Smeade, Stebbins, Tuffts, Weller, Williams. Of the group only one, John Stebbins, came through with his life. Four of the Hinsdells perished that day. So did the brave Captain Lothrop. Not one of the seventeen teamsters returned. In all, sixty-four men were massacred and later buried in a common grave nearby. The nameless stream was nameless no longer. Since that fateful, imprudent day, it has been known as Bloody Brook.

After this mortal blow, Deerfield was long untenable. Its bereaved survivors drifted southward and abandoned it to the Indians. The settlement sank back into the Pocumtuck wilderness. A few venturesome men returned in 1677 and started to rebuild, but eventually they were captured and carried to Canada, the first of many captives to follow that bitter trail. The canny French, perceiving in the Indians a valuable ally, soon promised cash rewards for English prisoners.

The indomitable tide would not be permanently stemmed, however. By 1682 the Proprietors of Deerfield were back in force. The town was rebuilt rapidly, and better fortified this time. The proud new citizens held their first town meeting in 1686. But apprehension had grown apace with the village once again. With the accession of William of Orange, hostilities between the French and English colonists became more bitter. Deerfield was conscious of the threat. Meeting House Hill was surrounded with a palisade of logs twelve to fourteen feet high. A small garrison was stationed in the village, but it added little to the sense of security. Deerfield was tragically vulnerable and its more thoughtful citizens were depressed by a sense of impending danger. Their minister, the Reverend John Williams, wrote on their behalf: "Strangers tell us that they would not live where we do for twenty times as much—the enemy having such an advantage of the river to come down upon us. Several say they would freely leave all they have, and go away, were it not disobedience to authority and a discouraging of their brethren."

The stamina and courage of the pioneer farmers were equal to the test. They did not "freely leave" all they had. They held on tenaciously for over twenty years and were rewarded by good harvests and a thriving village.

Dame Hannah Beaman, the gun-carrying school teacher, saw to it that the children received an education and trained them to scoot for shelter behind the stockade in case of danger. On one particular occasion they scampered just in time. This was on September 15, 1694, a day of proud victory for the fortified village and of humiliation for a certain French nobleman who had been adopted by the Abenaki Indians and had married the daughter of their chief. He was the Baron St. Castine, and his specialty was organizing bands of marauding Indians to carry on border warfare against the English. It was he who helped persuade the Indians to join the French army in an attack on Oyster River (Durham, New Hampshire) in which a hundred settlers were killed or captured. Encouraged by this success, the French gave St. Castine permission to attack another significant outpost—Deerfield.

The Baron and his Indians drew closer to the village on that September day and managed to escape detection by the guards on patrol. St. Castine's plan was to creep down a ravine, wade through an alder swamp and assault the north gate of the fort, but as the band left the ravine they were observed by Daniel Severance, a youth of sixteen. Although the boy was immediately shot, he gave his life in a noble cause. Men inside the fort heard the gunfire and had time to snatch their firearms and rush to the gate. Hannah Beaman, teaching her children on a home lot north of the spot where Daniel fell, also heard the shot. She herded her little flock together and with them made a mad dash for the stockade. The Indians plunged through the swamp in a vain attempt to cut them off. They were too late. As they fired a volley of bullets in her direction, Dame Beaman and her charges rushed through the gate to safety. The defenders of the fort, capably trained by Captain Wells, faced the Indians coolly and forced them to retreat into the wilderness. After this episode, Deerfield was given a brief, uneasy respite. Tension was ever in the air, but life went on, year after year. A fatal sense of security, lulled by false alarms, settled on the village.

When Queen Anne's War broke out, in 1702, Deerfield was still a northern frontier town along the Connecticut River and fearfully vulnerable to attack. Its citizens voted to repair the palisades, and appealed to the Boston government for financial aid. Settlers living outside the fortifications were encouraged to move in with their neighbors living within the fort. The next year only served to heighten the apprehension. In May the Governor of New York revealed that his Mohawk spies had discovered an expedition being formed near Montreal, with Deerfield as its objective. This information brought action from Governor Dudley in Boston, and twenty men were stationed in Deerfield as a garrison. Little episodes heightened the tension. In October two young Deerfield men, hunting outside the stockade for their cows, were captured by the red men and taken to Canada. The town was not only living on its nerves but in discomfort as well. Having a garrison meant that living quarters were cramped and food was short. From October until the next February, however, nothing occurred to alarm the people and they began to relax their vigil.

In that same interval Governor de Vaudreuil of Canada had organized an expedition consisting of 200 Frenchmen and 142 Abenaki and Caughnawaga Indians under the command of Major Hertel de Rouville, a distinguished

"The Dead of 1704"

officer in the service of New France. In the dead of winter he marched this army three hundred miles from the Sorel River, across Lake Champlain down the Winooski and Connecticut Rivers, and finally to Petty's Plain, an inland spot about a mile northwest of his objective, Deerfield. By the time he reached this point the French were half-starved and on the verge of mutiny, ready to surrender if the people within the fort offered much resistance. Tired and exhausted, de Rouville decided to rest there until a few hours after midnight when he moved his forces down the plain even nearer Deerfield.

Then, just before daybreak on that bitter cold night of February 29th, 1704, the blow fell. The stealthy horde of Indians and Frenchmen crept closer to the sleeping village, undetected by a faithless sentinel who had fallen asleep at his post. They came with a rush, now pausing to listen and again rushing forward, a maneuver calculated to mask their noise as gusts of wind. Four feet of drifted snow covered the ground to the height of the stockade and its crust was strong enough to bear the invaders. Entering the stockade without difficulty, they suddenly burst upon the sleeping villagers with hideous yells and flaming torches. The Indians were fiendish in their fresh war paint. They were bent on cold murder. In detached groups they broke into the houses, killing as they went. Sudden death awaited many a settler at his doorstep. Awakened in their beds and bound hand and foot, other victims were hurried half naked into the night. Hostages huddled together in the Meeting House and in Ensign John Sheldon's house on the Common. There, surrounded by the groans of the wounded and the wails of frightened children, they waited the dawn. The casualty list of that fearful night was a heavy one. Of the town's 291 inhabitants 48 were slaughtered and 111 were taken prisoner.

The best personal account of those tragic days was written by the Reverend John Williams, who came to Deerfield in 1686: "Not long before the break of day the enemy came in like a flood upon us, our watch being unfaithful. . . . They came to my house in the beginning of the onset, and by their violent endeavors to break open door and windows, with axes and hatchets, awaked me out of sleep; on which I leaped out of bed, and running toward the door, perceived the enemy making their entrance into the house. I called to awaken two soldiers in the chamber; and returned to my bedside, for my arms. The enemy immediately brake into the room, I judge to the number of twenty, with painted faces and hideous acclamations. I reached up my hands to the bed tester, for my pistol, uttering a short petition to God [then follows a quotation from Isaiah 38-10]. Taking down my pistol, I cocked it and put it to the breast of the first Indian who came up; but my pistol missing fire, I was seized by three Indians, who disarmed me, and bound me, as I was in my shirt; and so I stood for near the space of an hour." Two of the Williams children were killed, together with their Negro nurse. The minister and his wife, who had recently born her eleventh child, were taken prisoner with five surviving children. He continues the melancholy picture: "About sun an hour high, we were all carried out of the house, for a march, and saw many of the houses of my neighbors in flames, perceiving the whole fort, one house excepted, to be taken. . . . Upon my parting from the town, they fired my house and barn. . . . We went up the mountain, and saw the smoke of the fires in town, and beheld the awful desolations of Deerfield."

The one surviving house of which John Williams spoke was the largest and most impressive in the village, built about 1698 by Ensign John Sheldon and heavily fortified against attack. Its stoutly spiked front door withstood the assault for a time but finally the tomahawks ripped a gaping hole between its stout planks. Through this the Indians thrust a gun and fired at random, killing Mrs. Sheldon. The original door is still preserved in the village and constitutes the most dramatic reminder of that night.

A noble defense was put up by the inhabitants of the unfortified Benoni Stebbins house, where the attack fell later. Here seven men and a few women were able to ward off large numbers of French and Indians for three hours. By holding out so long, they prevented de Rouville from burning the town completely. Reinforcements from the south arrived about eight in the morning. They were joined by the few remaining Deerfield men and forced the invaders to withdraw. The French and Indians made an unexpected stand in the north meadows, however. Here they ambushed the English who in their fury had become overly reckless. Several Deerfield men were slain in this skirmish, bringing the total number of victims in the attack to forty-eight. A grim monument to them can be found in a corner of the Old Burying Ground today. There, under a single broad mound all forty-eight are buried in a single grave. A square stone is marked with the simple inscription: "The Dead of 1704."

An unspeakable ordeal awaited the luckless prisoners. Their captors forced them to march northward through the snow regardless of their age or health. For the ghastly trek of 300 miles which lay ahead they were given "Indian

"The Street" and the Old Indian House

shoes" and little else. The first night they camped in the Greenfield Meadows. A captive escaped and John Williams was warned that if others did the same the remainder would be burned. Marah Carter, three years old, was the first of the hostages to be killed. This was her penalty for straggling behind the party. Williams' own wife, Eunice, just risen from her sickbed, fared as tragically. While wading through the icy river she stumbled and collapsed half submerged on the rocks. She did not travel far after that. At the foot of the next mountain a bloodthirsty savage, with complete unconcern, slaughtered her with one blow of his tomahawk. Mary Brooks, heavy with child, was unable to keep pace with the Indians and confided in John Williams her belief that she would be killed, a prediction which came true on the same day. The pitiful procession shambled painfully northward, averaging eight miles on the third and fourth days. Finally they reached the West River where the enemy had left their dogs and sledges. With the wounded loaded on the sledges, together with the packs and some of the children, the pace was brutally accelerated. A dozen more women and children were unable to keep up and fell under the merciless hatchets of their tormentors. By the ninth day the survivors had reached the junction of the White and Connecticut Rivers. Here Major de Rouville separated them into smaller parties and ordered them to follow different routes northward. Thus they straggled piecemeal into Chambly, a few miles south of Montreal.

Not all of the prisoners were treated with such cruelty. An exception was little Eunice Williams, seven years old, one of the survivors of the Reverend Williams' children. Her captor carried her most of the way to Canada. Once arrived at his destination no amount of persuasion could induce him to give her up. The Governor of Canada offered him a hundred pieces of eight, but he refused. The little white girl became a member of the Indian tribe and married her captor at the age of sixteen. Apparently, she was happy, for many years elapsed before she consented to visit New England. Then in 1740, as a woman of forty-three, she returned to Deerfield, arousing great curiosity. She did not stay long. By that time she preferred the life of the Canadian Indians.

It is Parson Williams, once again, who recounts the most eloquent story of the captivity in Canada. In the book which has become an American classic, *The Redeemed Captive*, he tells of the valiant efforts of Ensign Sheldon, a survivor of the massacre, to trace the missing prisoners. "On the twenty-first of October 1704, I received some letters from New England, with an account that many of our neighbors escaped out of the desolations in the fort and that my dear wife was carried back and decently buried. . . . Not long after, Captain Livingston and Mr. Sheldon came with letters from his excellency, our governour, to the governour of Canada." The following August two more envoys, Mr. Dudley and Captain Vetch, arrived and carried on further negotiations. But it was not until the autumn of 1706, following Sheldon's third visit, that John Williams could write: "We came away from Quebec on October 25 . . . . and arrived in safety in Boston November 21; the number of captives 57, two of whom were my children."

In the meantime the stricken village made a forlorn attempt to carry on. More than half of the population had been driven over the snow to Canada, or lay beneath it. The remainder, about fifty men and women and some seventy-five children, mostly under ten, were tempted to abandon this outpost of civilization to the wilderness once again. They faced the future with more cheer, however, when the General Court of Connecticut stationed troops in Deerfield. The women and children were sent for a time to safer settlements, while the men remained to work their farms. The Frary house was intact and the Sheldon house had survived the incendiary torches of the Indians; moreover, soldiers were there to protect them, and the fertile meadowland was still theirs. The return of the lost captives was greeted by great rejoicing in the village. It bolstered the civic morale immensely. The grateful citizens built a new house for Parson Williams, who married his wife's cousin Abigail Bissell. The pioneer spirit flared anew and the village was once again on the road to prosperity.

Among the personal and poignant mementos of those frightful years that can still be seen in Deerfield is a book given Parson Williams by the Jesuit priests among his captors, in an attempt to win him away from his Protestant faith. This appropriately is in the home of one of his successors, Parson Ashley.

Stories of this period of Deerfield's history are legion. None appeals more to the imagination than the unverified but plausible tale about "The Bell of St. Regis." The story goes that a group of Caughnawaga Indians ordered a bell cast for their church. A foundry in France filled the order and forwarded the bell aboard a ship named the "Grand Monarque." The vessel was subsequently seized by the British who sold her cargo at a prize court in 1701 or 1702. As chance would have it, a Deerfield man, realizing that the Meeting House in his town needed a bell, purchased it. The bell was

brought to Deerfield, and after the French inscriptions and various insignia had been chipped off, it was hung in the Meeting House. The story continues that the Indians were enraged when they heard of this; first because their bell had been "stolen," and next because it hung in a Protestant church. There was nothing to do but undertake an expedition to recover it. This was accomplished on the night of February 29, 1704, and thus the bell found its way back to Canada. Is this fact or fiction? Researchers are combing records in the United States, Canada, England and France to try to find an answer.

Deerfield in its early days had indeed been a veritable "frontier of freedom" as England and France each strove to gain political control on this new continent. The assistance of the native Indians was eagerly sought by both, even though they frequently questioned the wisdom of such actions. A hitherto unpublished and unsigned proposal to abandon this course, following the 1704 attack by the French and the Indians, is among the archives of the Heritage Foundation. It reads in part:

". . . . And whereas here in North America the two above specifyed Colonyes of New France and New England, are under a sort of necessity in the time of war to make use of the natives of the contry (by the English called Indians and by the French more properly and justly called salvages) as auxiliary's—the marquis de VAUDREUIL, Governor of New-France and his Excellency, the honorable Joseph HUDLEY, Governor of New England . . . . have contracted, concerted and formly agreed that after the day to date of the signing of the following articles by themselves or any by them appointed that all hostilities what somever shall cease on both sides. . . ."

Deerfield's resurgence was rewarded by decades of comparative tranquillity. Hannah Beaman returned from captivity and began teaching school again, but had little use for her musket. The Indians were inclined to be friendly and cooperative. To maintain this peaceful state of affairs, an important meeting was arranged in Deerfield for the last week in August, 1735. It was attended by the Colonial Governor of Massachusetts, Jonathan Belcher and members of the General Court and by resplendent chieftains of four tribes—the Housatonic, Caughnawaga, St. Francois and Scaugacook. Hatchets were buried, pipes of peace were smoked and pledges of friendship were made. The interpreter was Joseph Kellogg, one of the captives of 1704, who spent ten years of his life as a member of the Caughnawagas. It is reported that the word he was asked most frequently to use was "Squawottuck," which, in the language of the Caughnawaga, means "more rum." On Sunday, August 31, the day following the conference, services were held in the Old Meeting House to ordain John Sergeant as Minister and Missionary to the Housatonic Indians in Stockbridge. An era of comparative friendliness was dawning. A few slight raids did occur and a lone farmer was not always safe in a remote field. The last real raid in the township occurred in 1746. More than two centuries of tranquillity since then have rewarded brave little Deerfield.

By mid-century the former outpost had become the center of a thriving wheat industry and an important cattle market. This meant a prosperity which was evident in several ways. A long overdue *joie de vivre* settled upon the village. Parties and dances were frequent and gay. A wedding was a major social event for the entire population. There were noticeable architectural changes along "The Street." The more primitive abodes of the early days were supplanted by gracious clapboarded houses in the best Connecticut Valley tradition. The remarkable and inherent good taste of these countrymen became evident in the furnishings of their houses. Some of the primitive furniture of early days gave way to handsome pieces made by Connecticut Valley craftsmen, or by noble examples imported from the mother country across the sea. Needless to say, this love of fine things, this appreciation of good craftsmanship, was not an attribute of this village alone. The whole period was one of discriminating good taste, both in the Colonies and Europe. It was an influence which seeped to the farthest outpost. Deerfield's hard-bitten farmers enjoyed beauty and amenities in their lives. They developed an instinctive eye for a good highboy, a fine mezzotint, a graceful decanter. They were eager purchasers of china and glassware, of silver and pewter and fabrics. They commissioned capable artists to paint their family portraits. They were willing buyers of fine furniture, particularly the work of the remarkable cabinet-makers who flourished in their own valley.

By a lucky whim of Providence, most of this era of good taste has been preserved until the present day, largely because of the vision and energy of certain Deerfield citizens. To Mr. and Mrs. George Sheldon, Miss C. Alice Baker, Miss Margaret Whiting, the Fuller, Williams, Wells and Hawks families and several others whose interest in the culture and decorative arts of the early days was unflagging, the present and future generations owe particular thanks. The charmed epoch has left countless reminders in the thirty or so eighteenth-century houses which are still preserved along the elm-vaulted street. Inventories, account books and old letters reveal how handsomely they were furnished. The indifference of the mid-nineteenth century, when fine furniture made way for the stolid Victorian comforts and the subsequent locust-like invasion of antique buyers, has made inroads into Deerfield's treasury of fine things, but, to judge by what remains and by what has been brought back, the village has had more than its share of good fortune. Loyal Deerfield citizens have passed their belongings down from one generation to another. Then, too, recent efforts by those who love the village and desire to portray accurately its eighteenth-century life have created a unique testimonial to the refinement and good taste of their forebears.

The life of leisure, good taste and dancing parties did not last long. Another cloud was already visible on the horizon. The struggle for independence began and split the village population into two camps. Divergence of opinion between the Whigs and the Tories became acute. Excited gatherings took place at the rival taverns, especially on the day when the weekly courier arrived on horseback from Boston. He stopped regularly at David Hoyt's Tavern to change horses before proceeding westward and he brought the latest news of the uprising. Hoyt's Tavern, a favorite of the local Tories, was installed in the historic Ensign John Sheldon's house—the same one which survived the incendiary torch in 1704. Sympathizers of the Crown also met in Catlin's Tavern farther down the street. The old Frary House had been converted into a Whig ordinary. Saxton's Tavern also became a chosen haunt of the Whigs. They had another rallying point in the general store run by David Field, a stalwart patriot who served as the Chairman of the Committee on Correspondence and Safety. Debate between the two factions became acrimonious on more than one occasion and led to occasional scuffles. A Deerfield citizen was accustomed to speak his mind freely. They still do!

The Tories were numerous and stubborn. Their most vocal and unyielding member was Parson Jonathan Ashley, who for decades had been the spiritual leader of the village. After the Boston Tea Party, with typical Tory defiance, he held a tea party and dance of his own to dramatize his sympathies. Parson Ashley was not one to abandon his convictions, even though some of his fellow Loyalists gradually left town or went over to the Whigs. Undaunted even when locked out of his own church and deprived of salary and firewood by the town, he refused to leave or to compromise. The sting of conscience seems to have influenced the village fathers when the old gentleman died in 1780. As a tardy atonement for their rough treatment they paid his executors a substantial sum "as arrearage in salary, firewood and rent of town lot."

News of the Boston Tea Party brought rejoicing to Deerfield's patriots. They determined to raise a Liberty Pole, a ceremony which was becoming increasingly popular in New England as resistance to the Crown grew. The pole was customarily a straight pine tree trunk some forty-eight feet in height, which could serve as a flagpole, a bulletin board where taunts to the Tories could be posted, and a rallying point for demonstrative Whigs. On July 28, 1774, they brought a newly felled tree to the selected spot adjoining patriot Field's store. But the young Tories of the village were on the alert. Led by Parson Ashley's son Elihu, they sawed the pole in two at night as it lay on the ground, a bit of malicious pre-Revolutionary horseplay which obliged the perspiring Whigs to search out another pine tree. The passions which flared elsewhere in the colonies seemed to strike an even brighter spark in Deerfield, a community which was long accustomed to fight for its existence. When a galloping messenger arrived in the village on April 20, 1775, and cried, "To arms! . . . Gage has fired upon the people . . . . Minute Men to the rescue!," the response was immediate. Once again the young men of Deerfield assembled on the Common, formed ranks and responded to roll-call, as their ancestors had answered Captain Lothrop almost exactly a century before. This time young Lieutenant Stebbins called the roll. Each man stepped forward as his name was called. They had the same familiar ring . . . . Henry Allen, Thomas Bardwell, Reuben Childs, Caesar Dickinson, Timothy Frary, John Hinsdale, Ariel Nims, Israel Nims, Oliver Smead, Samuel Smead, John Taylor, Neverson Warren, Jonathan Wells, Silas Wright. In the apt Gallic phrase, the more things changed, the more they remained the same!

Thus the flower of Deerfield's manhood fought for freedom once again, serving from Bunker Hill to Ticonderoga. The volatile village even declared *its* independence nine days before the Declaration of July 4, 1776. On June 25th of that year the town voted that it would, "if ye Honorable Congress shall for ye safety of ye United Colonies declare them Independent of ye Kingdom of Great Britain, solemnly engage with their lives and fortune to support them in ye measure."

During the Revolution, Deerfield assumed new importance as a cattle market. It became a veritable commissary for the American forces in the region. Among those who came to purchase meat in 1775 was Colonel Benedict Arnold, then a most respected patriot. He established himself at the Barnard Tavern (part of the Frary House), closed a deal for 15,000 pounds of beef and hurried on to Ticonderoga. Following the war, the town became an important center for raising stall-fed oxen. By this painstaking technique the animals were fattened for the markets in Boston and New York, where they fetched fancy prices. Cattle drovers made periodic visits to Deerfield, where they would argue at length with the local stock-raisers before settling upon a price. Then the long march to the abattoir would begin and the Deerfield citizen, considerably enriched, would seek new oxen to be fattened in his barns, many of which are still standing. But Deerfield was not destined to the life of a dull agricultural community. The advent of the steam locomotive was to provide overwhelming competition from the western plains, and to relegate the small New England farm to comparative obscurity. Nor was it to become the metropolis of the region. That distinction fell to Greenfield, three miles to the north.

Something different was due to befall the mile-long village in the meadows. A new influence made itself felt at the very end of the eighteenth century, an impetus which once again set Deerfield apart as an out-of-the-ordinary community. With worries of the war out of the way, the citizens began to consider a long-neglected subject, education. In 1787 fifteen of them grouped together as "Proprietors of the New School," built a school-house and obtained the services of Freegrace Reynolds, a recent Yale graduate as the first teacher. The school made a brave start, but the town fathers offered little or no support. After a few disappointing years another attempt was made. Deerfield's outstanding personalities—Major Seth Catlin, Colonel Joseph Stebbins, John Williams, Joseph Barnard and others—sought to obtain the Governor's signature on an act of the Legislature which would establish Deerfield Academy. The Governor signed willingly on March 21, 1797. The prospect of a new academy aroused understandable interest. The problem of selecting a site, a builder and a headmaster was confronted when the first meeting of the trustees of Deerfield Academy was held in the ball-room of the Barnard Tavern on April 18, 1797. It is significant that the trustees of the same Academy met in the same ballroom on April 18, 1947, precisely one century and a half later. The decisions of the first meeting were wise. The trustees bought a plot of land from Seth Nims and commissioned Asher Benjamin, then of Greenfield and later a noted Boston architect, to erect a two-story brick structure. In less than two years, on January 1, 1799, the Academy was formally opened. Enos Bronson had been selected as Preceptor. A notice in the *Greenfield Gazette* had given him, and the Academy, a dignified bit of advance publicity: "The Trustees of Deerfield Academy feel themselves happy in being able to announce to the Public that they shall be prepared to open said Academy on the first day of January next, having erected a convenient building for the accommodations of youth of both sexes and having provided a Preceptor who comes under the ample recommendations of the President and Professor of Philosophy of Yale College and of Dr. Dana of New Haven."

That year pupils came to the new Academy from forty-one towns. They varied widely in age, from eight years up. The rules were strict. Morning prayers were at five, or as soon as it was light enough to read. Boys and girls were not allowed to meet except at meals and prayers. Today's acknowledged values in the realm of co-education were scorned. If boys and girls walked together or visited on Saturday night or Sunday they were fined a dollar. There was also a dollar penalty for playing cards, backgammon or checkers, but the fine was only six cents for playing ball near the Academy. Another stipulation was: "No person shall attend to embroidery, painting, or any other of the ornamental branches to the neglect of the essential and fundamental parts of education." But the tuition fees offered more encouragement: "Admission charges for those instructed in reading, writing and English grammar, $2.17; for other branches of literature, $2.67. Board and room $1.50 per week." It is not surprising that the Academy prospered. The building had to be enlarged in 1810. It still stands today, with some alterations, as solid as ever, now serving as Memorial Hall, a museum of Deerfield's early history.

The fortunes of the Academy varied during the nineteenth century. Following a bequest by Mrs. Esther Dickinson in 1876, the seat of educational activity was moved to a site facing the Common. A new building was erected on this well-chosen spot in 1878. This was a rather forlorn period in American architecture, even though this building was one of the early attempts at classic revival and is mentioned in architectural books. Perhaps it is just as well for the aesthetic ensemble of Deerfield that the new building lasted less than fifty years. By the end of the century the Academy had hit a low ebb in attendance and equipment. A change was in order; a new face needed. Such problems had been solved before. Throughout the years Deerfield had been fortunate in having some bright young man, newly graduated from college, arrive on the scene and make a lasting imprint on the community. From Samuel Mather (Harvard, 1671) and Jonathan Ashley (Yale, 1730) on down to the present, the charm has held. So it happened that another young man fresh out of college (Amherst this time) arrived on the scene in 1902 and became the headmaster of the depleted little Academy. He came with fresh, new, invigorating ideas, and the energy to put them into effect. He believed in athletic sports for all of the student body, not just for the teams. From the moment of Frank Boyden's arrival, the Academy took on new vitality. Its faculty and students became a constructive force in the life of the town. The growth of the Academy in scholarship, in prestige and in the development of fine, healthy American manhood has been little short of phenomenal. In his more than sixty years as headmaster, the young man from Amherst seems to have lost very little of his youth. Under his wise and alert guidance, and with the constant help of Mrs. Boyden, Deerfield Academy has grown into one of the very finest, best equipped and most democratic preparatory schools in the land. Education has become the life of Deerfield today, largely because of its most eminent and most modest citizens, the Boydens.

Generations of schoolboys have been integrated into the life of Deerfield. They add to its population for a time and remain loyal to it in later years. They haven't had to tangle with the Indians, but neither have they faced a tranquil world. Deerfield's sons, both permanent and adopted, pursue the brave and often tragic path of their ancestors.

On the Common stands a red stone monument, topped by the familiar, somewhat outmoded, figure of a Union soldier leaning on his musket. In the War between the States another generation bearing the names of Allen, Barnard, Childs, Hawks, Hoyt, Saxton, Sheldon, Wells and Williams gave their lives. Inevitably, the enlarged community of Deerfield's sons, in and out of the Academy, paid a heavy price for freedom in both World Wars. A stroll through the village reveals other touching reminders—a tablet by the Town Hall, another in the Meeting House, a newly erected flagpole whose base is inscribed with the names of Deerfield's sons who gave their lives in World War II. Once again the descendants of the pioneers served their country. The names of Ashley, Allen, Childs, Ball, Arms and others appear once again on the roll-call, brave young men of today who proved worthy of a noble heritage. But the odds that faced their ancestors at Bloody Brook are not so overwhelming today. This time most of them returned safely.

The spirit and fortitude that made America are summed up in this cycle of sacrifice. In the crucible of daring and courage, exemplified by the sons and daughters of Deerfield, our country has been welded.

The first settlers who penetrated this wilderness brought an inestimable treasure within themselves . . . . the faith that burns in the hearts of free men. It is a treasure which has come down through generations and which in our time is more priceless than ever. In a wilderness of false gods, dubious standards, conflict, confusion and slander, the American people still retain this incomparable asset of their own making—the right to defend eternally their liberty under God.

Mezzotint of Governor Belcher

STRUCTURES ILLUSTRATED IN THE PHOTOGRAPHIC TOUR OF OLD DEERFIELD

FRONTIER OF FREEDOM

PART II

The perceptive camera, with the aid of captions, now assumes the narrative of Old Deerfield. In a village as photogenic as this, it is a pleasant undertaking. Beginning at the northern extremity of the village, the inquiring lens winds its way down the gracious old street, crossing some of its thresholds and peering into many of its backyards. The path of pictorial interest leads back and forth, but ever southward, making detours into two of Deerfield's modest side streets and ending at the edge of the south meadows.

Along the way the camera frequently goes indoors to obtain a closer glimpse of the life and tastes of Deerfield's early citizens. Many of these interiors can now be seen by the public—well over a hundred rooms. At the end of the book is a small portfolio showing some of the doorways, furniture and fireplaces which distinguish the village.

These pictures have been taken in all four seasons of the year, in varied moods of sun and foliage. Old Deerfield's pensive charm, however, has never been portrayed with more affection and understanding than by two ladies who bear an honored name, the late Misses Frances and Mary Allen. The photograph on Page 1 is reproduced as a tribute to these unassuming sisters who, in the early days of photography, recorded their native village with touching beauty.

A two-chimney dwelling, with a gambrel roof in front and a salt-box sweep behind, the Ashley House embodies the salient points of a good Deerfield house—unpainted clapboards, narrow windows and a rich doorway of the Connecticut Valley type.

The old Ashley house remained the family homestead until 1869, when it was moved to the rear of the property and converted into a tobacco barn. In spite of this indignity, it kept its noble bearing. This view, taken about 1900, shows the aged structure before it was restored to its former glory at the head of "The Street" and furnished in a manner consistent with Parson Ashley's taste and position.

Ashley House

For nearly half a century the village parson, Jonathan Ashley, lived in this weathered veteran which stands at the northern extremity of "The Street." He bought it in 1733 for the sum of 251 pounds when it was a comparatively new house. Here he performed marriages, officiated at funerals, and reared, with a certain amount of cooperation from Mrs. Ashley, a vigorous family of nine. He even took in boarders. Here also he gathered together the local Tories, for the parson was a consistent and often vehement supporter of the Crown. A member of a wealthy Westfield family, Jonathan Ashley was invited to the pastorate shortly after his graduation from Yale. A few years later he married Dorothy Williams, a preacher's daughter from Hatfield, and settled into the community with emphasis. Parson Ashley was a positive and outspoken personality, with strong religious convictions. He entered into an acrimonious controversy with his fellow Yaleman, Jonathan Edwards, on the problem of who was entitled to take Communion. He was a pungent and vigorous preacher, unhesitant in the defense of the mother country during the controversial days which led to the War of Independence. So fiery were his spoken sentiments that he found himself locked out of his church and pulpit on more than one Sabbath. Parson Ashley was one of the Tories to remain in the village during the Revolution. He lived on in this old house until his tumultuous days came to an end in 1780.

The central hallway of the Ashley house, one of the first of its kind in the village, is not symmetrical with the doorway. Its walls consist of thick vertical boards, paneled on both sides. The fluted urn finials and carved shell of the block-front Connecticut tall case clock resemble Newport products. The gate-leg table with molded ends is flanked by two vase-back chairs with a "Japanned" finish (allegedly having been sent to the Orient for decoration). The lantern is of the type known as a "Paul Revere lantern." On the wall is a mezzotint of Governor Belcher, who came to join Parson Ashley in Deerfield for a peace conference with the Indians in 1735. It is by J. Faber and bears the date 1734.

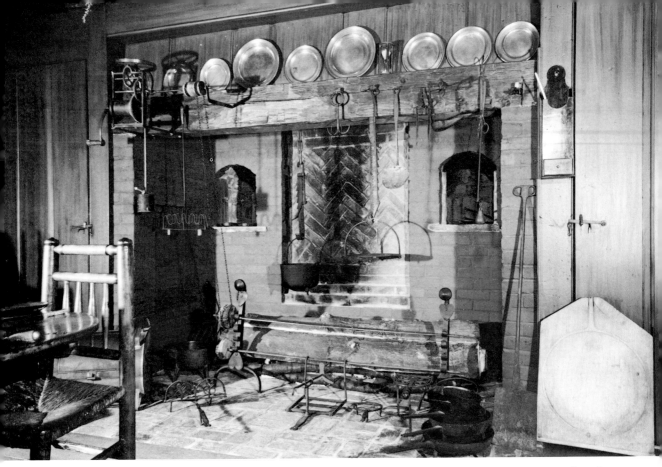

The kitchen of the Ashley house is built in the salt-box lean-to. Its magnificent fireplace is equipped to do all the cooking for a large family such as Parson Ashley's. A clock-jack turns the spits which rest on fine old fire-irons, each bedecked with two hearts.

In the end of the kitchen is a venerable corner cupboard containing a graduated sextet of pewter measures.

An unusual carved paneled pine cupboard with a shaped opening composed of reverse scrolls occupies one end of the kitchen. The chargers are English Delft. The table belonged to Parson Ashley when he lived in this house. It is set with a wooden bowl and plates and horn spoons. The lighting equipment here and throughout the Deerfield houses merits careful study.

26

A sophisticated note is struck in the north parlor, which was used for weddings, christenings and funerals as well as the parson's best company. The paneled walls are painted a soft lustrous blue, affording a dramatic background to the rich, golden yellow of the eighteenth-century satin covering the settee. The tea table is set with eighteenth-century china and the Chippendale chair is still adorned with the needlepoint made for it by Ann Saltonstall in 1742.

It is not difficult to picture a Colonial bridal couple standing before Parson Ashley, prayer book in hand, in the colorful, well-proportioned room. The bride, however, would have to compete with the beauty of the Queen Anne wing chair, whose covering of very fine American crewel on linen twill is a thing of startling grace and color. Both design and workmanship are typical of the American economy with thread. Infinite variety is achieved by the use of the same colors in different order. Four browns, four blues, four roses and a yellow are exquisitely blended in the following stitches: New England laid, chain, stem, French knot, crow's feet. The figures are never outlined.

Parson Ashley may have been a man of controversial opinions, but his good taste appears to be less debatable in view of the beautiful lowboy, an original Ashley piece in the parlor. This lowboy set a standard for the other furniture in the house. Above it sits a shelf clock made by Thomas Wilder of Hingham, dating from about 1780. Flanking it are two of the six New England Chippendale chairs in the room. The rug is an antique Kouba of Shirvan design. Reposing on the secretary in the parlor (above) is the

deed stating that this house was bought by Parson Jonathan Ashley in 1733 for the sum of 251 pounds. It appears probable that the house was built a year or two earlier by John Wells. On the desk are a needlepoint purse, a pair of old spectacles, a receipt signed by the parson in 1760 and a remarkable eighteenth-century brass inkstand, with a candle of its own. Its covered pots contain sand, ink and wafers and seals. Two Battersea enamel taper sticks stand on the small extending shelves.

The Chippendale block-front desk bookcase in the parlor of the Ashley house is one of the noblest in Deerfield. Its seasoned mahogany surface glows with a warmth that breaks into flame at the gilded finials. The shell-carved interior contains four secret drawers. A fifth secret compartment is artfully concealed in the pull rest for the writing top. The piece was made about 1775 for the Reverend John Marsh, then pastor of the church at Wethersfield, Connecticut. He became a chaplain in Washington's Army. Later it was owned by Marsh's relation, Richard Henry Dana, author of *Two Years Before the Mast*.

George the Third King of Great Britain

On the early New England cherry desk in Parson Ashley's study are books, pamphlets and sermons, some of the latter in Parson Ashley's own minute handwriting. Over the desk of this faithful Tory preacher hangs, appropriately enough, a portrait of George III. The print to the left is one of an issue done in Boston on December 22, 1755, the first historical print drawn and engraved in America. This is one of very few impressions known. It was drawn by an eyewitness, Samuel Blodget of Boston, of the Battle of Lake George, September 8, 1755, the day Colonel Ephraim Williams was killed there.

The inner walls of Parson Ashley's study are covered with pine paneling, unpainted but well waxed. During the winter months the house is far more comfortable than in the parson's day. All rooms are warmed by invisible radiant heat, an innovation which meets with a hearty welcome from antiquarians.

The mezzotint of the provocative George III is a fine one, having been done in London about 1760 by Myers.

The fireplace in the study is flanked by two enclosed cupboards. Two Pilgrim slat-back chairs, from the late seventeenth century, sit primly before the fire. Over the fireplace is a colorful bit of English stump work. The seventeenth-century trestle foot table with oval top is painted black, and is a very rare piece. The rug is an antique Oushak, woven in what is commonly known as a Holbein or Lorenzo Lotto pattern.

The piece of English stump work depicts Orpheus with his lute, surrounded by vividly illustrated animals, birds, insects and plants, with the sun and the moon above. All of nature is here under the spell of his music.

The north bedroom of the Ashley house is dominated by a handsome bed whose hangings of richly colored crewel work came from England. In the foreground, on an eighteenth-century gate-leg table of curly maple, are two of the parson's old ecclesiastical books and a wine glass which, according to family tradition, the parson emptied at his bedside each night. In the background is a Queen Anne dressing table, on which rests an old courting mirror. The rug is a Kouba and follows a Cabistan design.

The embroidery stand, with American crewel work in process, is something that was often seen in Colonial homes, though they are increasingly difficult to locate today. The chair to the right of the fireplace belonged to Dorothy Williams before she married the parson. On the daybed rests a turkey work cushion of bright colors. The portrait, by an unknown artist, is of Bithia Fogg, a distant relative of Governor Belcher. The tall chest is a Rhode Island piece.

The Connecticut sunflower chest is a piece that was made for a member of Mrs. Ashley's family. Its history can be traced back through the Williams and Billings families. The Bristol Delft posset cup and plates are flanked by a pair of pewter communion flagons of Connecticut origin.

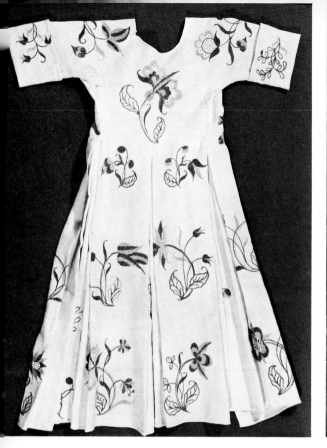

The dignity and charm of this locally made child's dress is evident. Appropriately, it is in the children's room in back of the chimney. It is worked in two shades of indigo linen thread on white linen. It has twenty-seven motifs showing effective use of stitches.

It is not difficult to understand why only a very few eighteenth-century rag rugs have survived. The loom of this rare example was warped with alternate green and unbleached wool, while the weft is of folded strips of cloth. The embroidery of roses, leaves and arabesques is done in rose, green and blue coarse crewels. This is seen in the south bedroom.

In the study hangs this oil portrait dated 1717 and signed J.C. It is one of a pair by the early eighteenth-century artist, J. Cooper.

The south bedroom is faced with unpainted sheathing and simply furnished. This is the children's room, and since the Ashleys had nine children (and took in boarders as well) it is not surprising to find a trundle bed squeezed in under the old pine folding bed. The folding bed with trestle feet is dressed with American crewel work made by one of the Ashley ladies. The wig stand is an eighteenth-century Deerfield item, and the wig cupboard with sliding doors deserves special note. The British uniform was taken from a British officer near Boston by a nephew of Parson Ashley, who was as rabid a "Whig" as the Parson was a "Tory."

The original frame of the gambrel roof is seen in the attic. The slot to the left has provoked many queries. It has been called by one modern humorist a slot for used razor blades, by more thoughtful observers an opening to shoot from, and just a plain air vent. In reality it is a bee trough for the convenience of the bees to reach the hive placed near the chimney in the winter.

Wright House

A century and a quarter ago there were four brick buildings in the village. The earliest was erected for Deerfield Academy, now the home of the local historical society (page 135). It was opened on New Year's Day, 1799. One member of the building committee was Asa Stebbins, who built the major portion of his own splendid brick house in the same year. When his son, Asa Stebbins, Jr., was married in 1824, the father planned and built for the bride and groom this house, known today as the Wright House, a name taken from that of the second owner. In the same year Asa Stebbins, as a forceful member of the committee planning the "Brick Church" (page 113)

diagonally across from his own brick house, was again a proponent of brick construction.

The Wright House faces the Ashley House at the north end of "The Street." The original brickwork, the shutters and the doorways with leaded lights within their arches exemplify in their design the good taste of this successful citizen of Deerfield. Even so, the commodious house had to be enlarged by a frame ell some years after its construction. The fence is a faithful reproduction of a former one, details of which were discerned from old pictures and careful research. The house contains many superb antiques, at present on loan from the George Alfred Cluett collection.

The formal "Chippendale Room" has red and gold
damask curtains with heavy gray and gilded wooden
valence boards. The mirror is one of two in the room.
The pie-crust table to the left, possibly of Connecticut
origin, is very rare, while other pieces portray the
formal influence of Philadelphia design. The rug is a
seventeenth-century Oushak.

In the parlor is a splendid half-round commode with
delicate inlay attributed to the Boston cabinet-maker,
John Seymour. It holds three pieces of Chinese export
porcelain. Over these hangs a portrait of George
Washington painted by Jane Stuart, in the manner of
her famous father, Gilbert Stuart.

The yellow painted walls and blue, star-patterned curtains in the music room serve as a gay setting for the exquisite gold and blue Federal mirror and the gold and white chandelier of carved wood. The pianoforte was made in 1796 by Broadwood & Sons of London, after designs by Thomas Sheraton, for Prince Don Manuel de Godoy, Prime Minister of Spain, as a gift from him to Queen Maria Louisa of Spain. It is inset with 111 Wedgwood and Tassie medallions and silver stars rimmed with ormolu. An ormolu royal coat of arms is on the side. The crown of Spain is depicted on the top by means of inlaid woods. A photograph of a contemporary engraving of this remarkable pianoforte hangs in the room.

The best available historical account of this unusual pianoforte seems to be that after the presentation to Her Majesty, the Queen of Spain, it may have been looted during the Napoleonic Wars. It came up for sale in the Leverhulme collection in New York in 1926, and was bought by George Alfred Cluett as a gift to one of his daughters.

The shelf clock is by Simon Willard. The base has a black, white and gold *"églomisé"* coat of arms of the Apothecary Guild. Above the design appears in Latin *Tempus Rerum Imperator* ("Time Conquers All Things") and below are the words *Opiferque per orbem dicor* ("I am called a helper throughout the world").

This dining room, with gray woodwork and cheerful
yellow silk curtains surmounted by swag valences, contains a beautiful English needlework rug and remarkable furniture. The tables (attributed to Seymour)
under each window are, to be sure, appropriate neighbors for the small secretary at the left. This is one of
the two known pieces bearing the label of John Seymour of Boston. The Brookfield, Massachusetts, dining table, the mirror (one of a pair in the room) and
the clock deserve notice.

The girandole clock by Lemuel Curtis (1790–1857)
is probably one of about twenty-five ever made. The
table below the clock resembles in many details those
made by the Seymours of Boston, but bears the remains
of a label of Todd & Adams, Cambridge Street, Boston, Massachusetts.

The mantel in this bedroom and others in the Wright House extend beyond the chimney breast, a feature seen also in the Asa Stebbins House. Over the mantel is the portrait of an unknown but charming lady by a yet unidentified artist, who may be Theus. The clock by Simon Willard on the table was patented and probably made in 1822. It is popularly known as a "Lighthouse" clock. The chest at the right and the desk bookcase at the left were until recently owned by a family in Deerfield, and were probably made by a local craftsman. The rather ornate character of these pieces shows an extraordinary regard for detail. From the carved bracket feet to the delicate bird, one sees an exquisite, even if overdone, mastery of the tools of the trade. The fluted quarter-columns terminating in a triple-layered grouping of acanthus leaves turn out as the door is opened.

The curtains in this room are a red moreen. The large rug is an unusually beautiful Indian seventeenth-century one, reduced from a larger rug possibly used in the Jaipur Palace. It is considered a precious specimen of the great art of India. The chairs are both by Newport craftsmen.

(Left) The inlay, the fretwork, the full swag and the terminal rosettes of the scroll pediment of this desk-bookcase all indicate the desire of this local craftsman to portray every skill in his repertory.

The Massachusetts bed dressed with crewel work has a heavy claw-and-ball foot and removable kneecaps, These coverings at the knees were a method of hiding the bolts.

Beyond the Wright House at the north end of "The Street" lie the green, open meadows so well known to the Deerfield pioneers.

This smiling white house has passed through many ownerships and remodelings. The land once belonged to Mehuman Hinsdell, the first white child born in Old Deerfield (1673), who willed it to his son, Colonel Ebenezer Hinsdell. They were a valiant family, for there were four Hinsdells in Captain Lothrop's ill-fated company. Some of them drove the ox-teams. The autumnal view demonstrates that not all of "The Street's" elms are old. Victims of old age are assured of young replacements. Another well-known family, the Ebenezer Williamses, owned the house in 1816. It has been lived in by three generations of the Cowles family.

The BARDWELL-STEBBINS HOUSE is a picture of dignity standing on a knoll above "The Street" and sheltered by its colossal elm. Samuel Bardwell built the house, probably in 1771, and ran it as a tavern. Dennis Stebbins, who had the reputation of making the best brooms in the Connecticut Valley, and had five daughters to help him in his craft, bought the house in 1799. It was restored about 1907. Its narrow front hallway with a double stair is unique in Deerfield.

A handsome French landscape paper, probably applied in 1816, adorns the parlor walls of the Hinsdell house, shown on the opposite page.

Sheldon-Hawks House

The Sheldon-Hawks House is a study in dark weathered tones. Its narrow windows, capped with pediments on the façade, are a hallmark of Deerfield architecture. This is the birthplace of George Sheldon, author of the authoritative *History of Deerfield* and founder of the local historical society, the Pocumtuck Valley Memorial Association. The present house was built in 1743, and the rear wing was added in 1802, but this home lot goes back to 1708. The dwelling was later lived in by a relation of George Sheldon, Susan Hawks, and it has borne the name Hawks from the early twentieth century. A stone marker informs us that it was handed down from sire to son, "the longest holding of any estate by a single Franklin County family." It is adorned with a doorway in the best Connecticut Valley tradition. Its moldings are rich, and its original double doors are restrained. Time has stained the entire surface of the house a fine tobacco brown.

An autumnal view of the Sheldon-Hawks House, with the Ashley House in the distance.

In the north parlor of the Sheldon-Hawks House one sees many furnishings that were in Deerfield in the eighteenth century, among them the Dickinson family clock and three Barnard family Chippendale chairs. The block-front desk of Massachusetts origin has heavy claw-and-ball feet. The portrait by Sir Nathaniel Dance, an English painter who influenced American eighteenth-century artists who came to England, depicts an unknown gentleman in a yellow coat. The rare Oushak rug (seventeenth century) is medium-sized and woven in unusually soft red, yellow and blue tones.

The eighteenth-century practice of having a bed in a parlor is followed in the corner of the north room. The canopied bed has rich, golden yellow hangings. Their design and color are repeated in the window curtains.

Let us introduce you to two charming young ladies—the Buell sisters of Litchfield, Connecticut. Ralph Earl had the privilege of painting them in 1802. Done in his typical manner, with the rolling hills of the Connecticut countryside as a background, Earl has caught one sister in a meditative mood about to munch an apple, while the other (opposite) may be reading her diary, for the pages appear full of words more in the nature of handwriting than set type. Both portraits are signed and dated by the artist.

The south parlor, or dining room, is note-worthy for its wide paneling, probably un-painted when the house was first built. To the left of the fireplace hangs the member-ship certificate of Dr. David Townsend in the Society of the Cincinnati. It is signed by George Washington as President and General Henry Knox as Secretary. The small pictures are original designs by the French artist Jean Pillement, who married an English girl named Allen. The family connection with the Allens of Deerfield has not been established.

The curtains are a delicate blue, which blends with the Leeds-type bowl and plates and with the Delft on the Massachusetts marble-top table at the right. In the corner are a seated figure wearing a brocaded dress probably designed by Pillement and a standing figure wearing a white brocade gown with startling blue flowers.

The blue and white dress shows in greater detail in this view of the south parlor. The rug is an eighteenth-century Kouba with an Ispahan motif. The Ralph Earl portraits of the Buell sisters are seen in this room.

Three pieces of the Chinese export tea set sent by Major Shaw to his friend, Dr. David Townsend, are shown in this picture, which reveals well the delicacy of the design. The shallow cupboard which contains them (page 171) is just deep enough to hold teapots or cups, but not a plate laid flat. Each piece bears the insignia of the Society of the Cincinnati, an eagle with a medal on its breast. The cipher of David Townsend, to whom it belonged, is also on each piece. Very few sets of the Cincinnati porcelain were made, and still fewer exist today. The set is truly a thing of beauty. In addition to the eagle and medal, the decoration consists of bordering and sprigs of flowers. All features are done in the finest detail. Of the original thirty-nine pieces listed, thirty-four are now in Deerfield.

Also preserved is the membership certificate of David Townsend and his book on the Rules and Regulations of the Massachusetts Society, as well as his portrait and the original letter written by Major Shaw who sent the tea set to Dr. Townsend. The letter reads:

"Accept, my dear friend, as a mark of my esteem and affection, a tea set of porcelain, ornamented with the Cincinnati and your cypher. I hope shortly after its arrival to be with you, and in company with your amiable partner, see whether a little good tea improves or loses any of its flavor in passing from one hemisphere to the other. Interim—believe me always,

Yours,
S. Shaw

Canton in China
20 Dec. 1790"

The ladies who lived in this house in the eighteenth century were known as "sempstresses," experts with the needle, who made dresses for their neighbors. Consequently it seemed appropriate to have a room arranged in their honor. In the hanging corner cupboard are pewter buttons, skeins of wool and other things useful to the sempstresses. This, too, was the room where George Sheldon wrote his celebrated history of Deerfield.

In the kitchen the ample cooking arrangements, the pair of blanket racks, the settle and the livery cupboard behind it portray a comfortable approach to life. A folding bed was also kept in the corner of this warm kitchen.

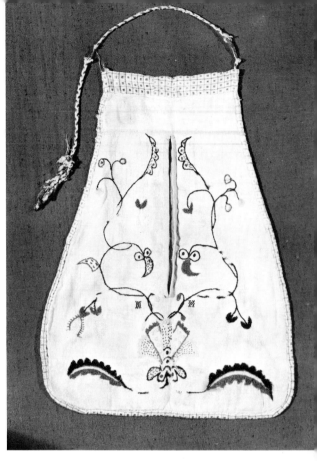

Women living near ports or large cities could buy their crewels in light skeins like these as they came off ships from abroad. This small eighteenth-century workbag (above) is embroidered in crewels. In towns like Deerfield the general practice was for the needlewoman to card, spin and dye the threads herself.

Tied around a lady's waist by tapes, these pockets (upper right) hung beneath her skirt and proved very practical. Usually made of linen, dimity, twill or sometimes scraps of pieced material, the edges were frequently bound with calico. The decoration was free, varied and sometimes bore the owner's or maker's initials. This example, composed of several types of stitches, is of dark-and-medium blue, and was made by Molly Johnson Hawks of Deerfield.

Another view of the sewing room (opposite) shows evidences of early needlework even in one of the framed pieces on the walls.

The upper chamber is one of the most colorful rooms in Deerfield. The bed is dressed with brilliant flame stitch hangings, while the curtains and chair coverings are a red moreen. The walls are painted a delicate yellow, while the paneled wall is a mellowed dark pine. The rug is a Karabagh.

The south chamber is primitive compared with the north room. Here, too, the pine paneling has never been painted. The folding bed is covered with an India print, while on the wall is an embroidered hanging with many figures in gay colors. If they could speak and tell their story, perhaps they could solve the mystery of the provenance of this intriguing piece.

The mellowed pine walls of the north upstairs chamber are truly magnificent in their original unpainted condition, even though the bolection moldings retain the ineradicable mark of the position of a wall which divided this fine chamber into two smaller bedrooms. As in many Deerfield houses, the north rooms, especially upstairs, were of better architectural design than the south rooms. No completely satisfactory explanation has been found. One would-be authority has concluded, to his own satisfaction at least and his pleasure in explaining the mystery, that when the house was first built the family moved in with little money or time to embellish the warmer southern rooms. When more affluent times came and the oldest son brought home a bride, the north chambers were built with more elegant paneling.

The oil portrait over the fireplace is of Stephen Greenleaf by John Wollaston. Greenleaf was the last Colonial sheriff of the Massachusetts Bay Colony.

Securely seated on its eminence above "The Street," this dignified house was built about 1783 by David Dickinson, a major in the American forces during the Revolutionary War. One of the many children who grew up in the rural calm of the DICKINSON HOUSE was George H. Houghton, who became rector of the far-from-rural "Little Church around the Corner" in New York.

The doorway, a later alteration, has the sidelights often seen, but the ceiling of the hallway was too low to permit a properly proportioned fanlight above. Consequently, by an ingenious combination of moldings and paint, the effect of such a design was achieved.

Silver Shop

One of the many preservation projects in the village is the Clesson House, which was returned to its original site, restored and adapted to the uses of the "Parker and Russell Silver Shop . . . at the sign of the Silver Fork."

In 1814 Joseph Clesson erected, as it turned out, the first and only part of the house, a small two-story, gambrel-roofed ell for a larger house he planned to build facing the street. This plan was never consummated, probably on account of his death two years later. This section passed through various hands until 1872, when it was moved to a location east of the present state highway to Greenfield. In 1960, eighty-

eight years later, it was moved back to the original site.

Here the craft of a silversmith is demonstrated, and there is a display of early American silver. It has been generally understood that some members of the Burt family, prominent silversmiths of Boston, had lived in Deerfield. Ebenezer Wells was known to have worked at the trade too. However, Isaac Parker, who moved to Deerfield in 1774, and his apprentice John Russell, a native son of the village, can be considered to have been the founders of a long line of silver and cutlery craftsmen whose art has been perpetuated in the area ever since.

Even though the walls and ceilings of the west room have new plaster, and radiant heat has been installed, all the woodwork, from which modern coats of paint were removed, is original, as are the floorboards. The fan-like folds in the four corners over the mantel frame are an attractive feature. The portrait is of Benjamin Cook, a Northampton, Massachusetts, silversmith of the late eighteenth and early nineteenth centuries. The needlework over the painted chest was done by a nine-year-old girl named Elioner Forester.

Beyond the front windows of this room there would have been constructed the larger and main body of the house, conforming to the plan common to so many of the houses on "The Street." The Aaron Willard, Jr., banjo clock of generous proportions (four feet, eight inches high) is unusual. The curtains are made from an old linsey-woolsey spread that had seen better days.

The forge was copied from the one originally used by Nathan Storrs and Benjamin Cook in Northampton. Nearly all of the tools of many and varied types are of eighteenth-century vintage. They were obtained in England, Boston and Williamstown, Massachusetts.

The adjustable candle-holder and the cut-out section of the workbench with the hanging apron to preserve particles of falling silver for future use show the care and necessarily practical features of the silversmith's daily work, which is still demonstrated here.

A fireproof wing of cinder-block construction, covered with old boards, was added in the rear. It was hidden from the street by judicious planting, which included the preservation of old trees. This wing houses the silver collection which the Heritage Foundation has been forming for many years. Old paneling with faded green paint and the original doors of the two closets were installed at the fireplace end of the room. The closet at the left houses a collection of spoons made by New England silversmiths. The one at the right displays a very rare set of smaller tools for chasing and the like, with the original touchmark of John Staniford of Windham, Connecticut, as well as silver by Cook and other Connecticut Valley makers. The furniture in all three rooms is basically the early or unsophisticated type of the seventeenth and eighteenth centuries.

Glass cabinets surrounded by paneling were built to house the showcases along one wall. Several fine silver pieces, originally owned by Deerfield people, are on display. These have joined many other examples of the silversmith's art, including items a silversmith would have been called in to work on or repair.

The paneling around the fireplace in the workshop is the original. The bricks were also originally used in this chimney, though in the interim they were built into the walls of a house erected on this site.

This group of silver pieces are some of the many owned in Deerfield in the early days. The casters are by Paul Revere. The tankard, with the initials of various members of the Williams family, bears the touchmarks of Jeremiah Dummer (Massachusetts, 1645–1718). The two cups belonged to two Stebbins sisters, and the spoon, one of many on exhibition, was made by John Russell of Deerfield, who also owned the scales sold by Joseph Richardson of Philadelphia (as the label on the box says).

The Silver Shop on a bright spring afternoon.

Old Indian House

This darkened wooden house with an overhanging second story and a Connecticut Valley profile is not old, but a reproduction of the house which Ensign John Sheldon built in 1698. It was then the most imposing house in the village and stood near the Church. The peril of Indian attacks was great. On the fatal night of February 29, 1704, the Old Indian House was able to resist the attack of the savages until its stoutly spiked front door gave way to the blows of the tomahawks. Then the Indians fired at random through the slit in the door, killing ·Mrs. Sheldon. Taking possession of the house, they used it as a depot for their captives and set fire to it upon leaving with their hapless prisoners. However, the flames were extinguished and the bereaved Sheldon lived on in the house when he was not making trips to Canada to redeem the Deerfield captives.

During the early days of the Revolution, David Hoyt ran the Old Indian House as a tavern. It served as a Tory headquarters, just opposite the Saxton Tavern which was the gathering place for the Whigs. The village Common was the scene of many a scuffle between the two. The Indian House could have been saved in 1847. One of the first known American preservation efforts to try to save it took place that year, but the money could not be raised and the Indian House was dismantled the following year. Its battered door and other mementos are preserved in Memorial Hall. The present reproduction was made in 1929 and presented as a gift by William H. Abercrombie, in memory of the Deerfield pioneers.

The Colonial kitchen of the Indian House has several massive components—a summer beam of large dimensions, a fireplace accommodating husky logs and copper cauldrons. This may have been the taproom.

A discreet note of red is added to "The Street" by the SALT-BOX HOUSE, a small structure with wide-spaced windows and a handsome doorway. It comes from the nearby town of Conway, where it was threatened with destruction, and replaces a more recent house of gingerbread persuasion.

Allen House

Mrs. Mary Bunker first drew the lot on which this distinguished farmhouse was built. It was sold in 1687 to Simon Beaman, a garrison soldier whose wife, Hannah Beaman, was the first school teacher in the frontier settlement. As early as 1694 she ran a "dame" school near this spot. The Beamans began to build their house here, but it was burned to the ground during the massacre of 1704. The courageous couple was captured by the Indians and led off through the snow to Canada. But they were back in Deerfield the next year, building their house anew. This is the structural heart of the present Allen House. Hannah Beaman sold it in 1722 to Thomas Bardwell, who brought with him his bride, Sarah. Soon they were adding a lean-to to accommodate a growing family, in whose hands it remained for close to a century. Bardwells married Allens, and the name of the old house shifted. About 1835 the central chimney was replaced by two small ones separated by a central hall. In recent years the house has been restored by its present owner. The central chimney is back in place. So is the double door—with the unspoken blessing of Bunkers, Beamans and Bardwells. It is a story which can be told and retold, with slight variations, all along Deerfield's eloquent street. This house is not open to visitors.

A fresh fall of snow throws reflected light on the Allen House, brightening its sober sides.

The first flush of springtime finds the Allen House framed against diaphanous foliage, its weathered clapboards contrasting with the early forsythia. Jonquils are out, and the long winter is forgotten.

65   The living room of the Allen House reflects the opulence and good taste of Deerfield's frontier farmers during the less rigorous days preceding the Revolution. The furnishings are consistent with this period.

The living room of the Allen House is a striking demonstration of the comfort and charm of eighteenth-century American furnishings. The walls of this room, in common with others in the house, are made of beautiful pine sheathing. Before the recent restoration, they were covered with lath and plaster, as was the beamed ceiling. This is a colorful room. From the eighteenth-century yellow damask curtains to the green wing chair and oriental rugs there is a constant play of harmonious tones.

The inner wall of traditional vertical feather-edged boards serves as a warm background for two pastels and a bead picture of a Biblical subject. To the left of the huge fireplace, which was formerly used for cooking, is a fine Rhode Island pole screen with an American embroidery picture known as "The Fishing Lady of Boston Common." The brass candlesticks and other gleaming metals lend sparkle to this cheerful room.

Two magnificent pieces adorn the east walls of the living room. The chest and secretary were made for a bride and groom about 1781, according to an early handwritten note pasted in the door of the secretary. Authorities agree that these are Connecticut pieces, probably the work of either Aaron Roberts, Benjamin Burnham or Samuel Loomis. The corner chair of San Domingo mahogany has the original slip seat of needlework bearing the date 1772 and the name Polly Wright worked into the design. The straight chairs are by the Chapins of Windsor, Connecticut. The horizontal wallboards indicate that this was originally an outside wall before the lean-to addition was added to the rear.

In the dining room, the beautifully turned legs and stretchers of the early gate-leg table demonstrate the flair for beauty manifest in the life of the colonists and the expert skill of their early craftsmen. The table is set with pewter, some of which was made by Samuel Pierce of Greenfield. Above the table hangs a pewter chandelier, one of the two on display in the village. Many table implements, such as graters and cutters, the latter for use on the conical sugar loaf, add a sense of the living past. The claw-and-ball foot wing chairs are upholstered with colorful eighteenth-century needlework. To the left of the fireplace is one of the rare engravings of the Boston Massacre by Paul Revere, and beneath it is a water-color done by an eight-year-old boy in 1776, depicting his idea of Paul Revere's historic ride. Above the wide oak lintel are two cupboards, one discreetly closed, perhaps to hide the host's bottles.

The dining room is enriched by crewel work hangings and a commodious twelve-sided, drop-leaf table. The Queen Anne vase-back chairs are covered with their original needlework slip seats. A marble-top serving table and a delicate tea table in the left corner, an unsymmetrical pine corner cupboard, oriental rugs and a unique New England wax sconce between the windows all add to the beauty of this hospitable room. The downstairs bedroom fireplace deserves particular attention for its display of three examples of needlework and the bright salt glaze wall pockets.

The ground floor bedroom of the Allen House sacrifices neither comfort nor authenticity. The desk is an eighteenth-century piece owned by the Allen family, having recently been presented to the Heritage Foundation by a lady who purchased it directly from this property in the early days of this century. The bed and other pieces are also of Deerfield provenance. The blue and white English toile is signed and dated "Jones 1761." The chairs are covered with a delicate crewel.

The diminutive chest with heavily scrolled top is one of the gems of the Deerfield furniture collection.

The small Chapin desk-bookcase shows, in the delicate central cartouche finial, the influence of Philadelphia design on this Connecticut maker, for he worked under the noted craftsman Savery in the City of Brotherly Love.

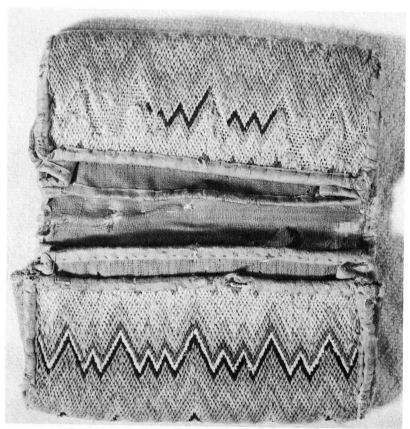

Wallets were frequently embellished with embroidery, not alone for beauty but because this also made them more durable. This one is lined with vermilion cambric and bound with an olive-green ribbon. The flame stitch on canvas is wrought in shades of blue, yellow, green, red and brown.

The pictures of the Hogarth room tell the story of one of the most interesting rooms in Deerfield. This room, however, is seldom seen, because the Allen House, which contains these treasures, is not yet open to the public. The pine wall sheathing and the floor are made of beautiful old boards of astonishing width. This warm background sets off the English crewel work curtains and the rare Holbein pattern Oushak rugs, as well as a splendid collection of Hogarth color prints and two Copley portraits of the Reverend and Mrs. Arthur Browne of Portsmouth, New Hampshire, painted probably about 1756. The room also contains a collection of "Spanish foot" furniture.

The furnishings of the north second-floor room are of a less sophisticated style than the other rooms in the Allen House. The easy chairs, table and painted chests are brought out in a brilliant manner by the gay red curtains, caught up in an authentic yet infrequently used knot.

The painted chest in the upstairs chamber was made before 1720. It is decorated with a tulip design and is of a type attributed to Charles Gillam of Saybrook, Connecticut. On the paneling are the telltale marks of the lime which has eaten into the pine when some owner covered the original woodwork with lath and plaster.

The bed dressing was worked by the grand-daughter of the Reverend John Williams, whose mother was taken as a captive to Canada in 1704. The pattern here alternates small plants with fruit trees, in contrast to the more usual early New England coverlet pattern of a single branching tree or vine. Here rose, carnation, tulips and berries all grow happily from the same root.

The English crewel work curtains show up well in this view of the Hogarth room. Over the early desk on frame is a portrait said to represent a member of the Saltonstall family. Fine old Delft pieces grace the table in the foreground.

No house in Deerfield has a more spacious setting than the THOMAS DICKINSON HOUSE. Joseph Barnard, who had the double distinction of being the first Town Clerk and of having the oldest gravestone in the burying ground, lived on this lot as early as 1685. The present house was built by Thomas Dickinson about 1752. It is sometimes known as the Mulberry House because of the mulberry trees that once grew on the property.

The appendages of the Thomas Dickinson House—smokehouse, wagon shed, and gambrel-roofed ell—stretch out in the snow, overshadowed by the massive bulk of ancient elms. The old chimneys veer noticeably from the vertical.

The **JOSEPH STEBBINS HOUSE** is opulent, both in architectural detail and in size. Even a fourth-story attic window squeezes in under its commodious roof. It follows the two-chimney, central-hallway plan. Wooden quoins frame its white clapboards. This imposing mansion was built about 1772 by the distinguished soldier and patriot, Joseph Stebbins. He began his career as a Lieutenant of Minute Men, was Captain under Colonel Prescott at the Battle of Bunker Hill and later became a Colonel of Militia. His thirteen children were born here. There was plenty of room for them under this broad gambrel roof.

This white house, now serving as a part of the BEMENT SCHOOL, is another early Deerfield edifice. The house in the background, known as the Barton House, was built about 1805.

The Joseph Stebbins House rejoices in two fine doorways. This one, facing "The Street," is very English in feeling, even to the subtle entasis of the pilasters, but its five arched lights bear the sure mark of the Connecticut Valley.

In the foreground of this snowy view of "The Street" is the Bement School, a co-educational boarding and day school founded in 1925 for children ranging in age from six to fourteen. The house, which has ample wings and additions, was an old one repaired in 1825. An earlier owner of the property was Zadock Hawks, tanner and currier, who was blessed with two sons, named Zur and Zenas. Zenas had a shoe shop in the back of this house. This digression is admittedly due to the novelty of their given names.

The ell of the PINK HOUSE dates from before 1757. One of Old Deerfield's most ardent patriots, Colonel David Field, lived to the south of this house, and had a store on the present vacant lot. He was a delegate to the Provincial Congress in 1775 and the Constitutional Convention (1779–1780). His store was a gathering place for the Deerfield Whigs, and it was logical to erect the Liberty Pole in front of it. Colonel Field, as Chairman of the Committee of Correspondence, Inspection, and Safety, did valiant work in keeping in touch with Boston and other towns. The feud between Whigs and Tories continued until the Revolution began in earnest. Then many of the Tories either became Whigs or left town.

The WILLIAMS-BILLINGS HOUSE is a sunny, white structure built between 1740 and 1750. Here lived Dr. Thomas Williams, brother of Ephraim Williams, founder of Williams College. Today a prime function of "The Street's" sidewalks is to provide safe speedways for the tricycles of the young.

Asa Stebbins House

Following the frightful massacre of 1704, most of the Deerfield survivors were financially unable to rebuild their homes except on a modest scale. Many of them were content to build simple one-story houses, remodeling and adding new sections as their fortunes improved. About 1750 Joseph Stebbins, Sr., the father of Asa Stebbins, was probably living on the southern side of this lot. He was a shrewd and versatile businessman. When Old Deerfield became a center for beef cattle during the Revolution, he seized the opportunity to furnish leather equipment for the army.

Reverend William Bentley made the following entry in his diary in August, 1793, regarding a return visit to Deerfield after an absence of five years: "The condition of this town is little changed. In the street are some of the richest Land holders in New England. The Meeting House is now painting. There is a public Clock, a lantern upon the Dome, & a fine appearance of the private buildings. Here I was obliged to stop & remember my former acquaintance. Mr. Hoit at the Tavern waited upon me to visit

Mr. Stebbins, aet. 74 (the father of Asa Stebbins), with whom I once boarded. He is the richest farmer in Hampshire County & began by his industry in Shoemaking, Tanning, &c. I visited the Houses of Messieurs Dickenson, &c. but found almost all the men absent in the meadows. foun Deacon Armes, Esqr Sexton, Esqr Williams, Col. Stebbins, &c."

Joseph Stebbins' son, Asa, apparently inherited his father's large savings and his business as well. His older brother, Colonel Joseph, Jr., had earned such a fine reputation at Bunker Hill and Saratoga that the town allowed him to erect a grist mill that was to be forever tax-free "so long as water runs and grass grows." He and Asa formed a partnership and were so successful in this venture that the latter was able to build the imposing brick front section of the house in 1799. There is a possibility that the bricks were made on the very lot where the house now stands. The rear was originally a simple gambrel roof structure with dormer windows. At a later date (*circa* 1879) a full second story was added and the roof line changed to a pitched roof.

This view of the central hallway of the Asa Stebbins House shows the graceful, free-flowing stairway, a characteristic design of Asher Benjamin, of which all too few remain. The French paper on the walls depicts "Captain Cook's Voyages." The portrait at the right is of Captain Robert Stoddard (1719–1776), painted by John Greenwood (1727–1792).

The south parlor of the Asa Stebbins House is perhaps the most sophisticated room of its period in Deerfield. The mantelpiece and its mirror, the crystal chandelier and the original garlanded, plasterwork cornice all contribute to what might be called its light-hearted formality. On the table is an English pink lustre tea set marked "Wood," once used in Greenfield.

In the south parlor is a portrait of Robert Stoddard, painted by Gilbert Stuart in 1775 when the artist was but nineteen years of age. It is still in its original frame.

For years the Asa Stebbins House was considered one of the show places of the village. This is not surprising in view of the opulence of its south parlor. Some delicate pink substance was mixed with the plaster that covers the walls of this room. An Aubusson rug echoes the same tonal pattern. The corner table (its mate is in the opposite corner) is attributed to Thomas Howard of Rhode Island. A third table, in the foreground, may be the work of Abraham Forster of Charlestown, Massachusetts. The pargeted ceiling dates from the early nineteenth century. On the table in the foreground are a creamware cake basket and pierced covered dishes, flanked by two rare agate candlesticks with silver mountings.

The windows of the south parlor are adorned with mull curtains, crowned with pink, blue and gold brocade swags held up by gilded wooden crescents. The roll-top desk between the windows has been attributed to the Seymours of Boston.

The central hall of the Asa Stebbins House is brightened by a handsome six-paneled door with a semicircular fanlight. The grandfather clock is by David Wood of Newburyport, Massachusetts. This wallpaper has since been replaced by a paper known as "Captain Cook's Voyages."

The rich red satin curtains and red-toned Aubusson rug in the north parlor complement the green walls which faithfully follow remnants of the original color, discovered after removing several layers of Victorian wallpaper. Two easy chairs (familiarly known as "Martha Washington" chairs) are on either side of the Seymour tambour secretary. The portrait is of a Dr. Dudley, painted by Samuel Waldo.

Another view of the north parlor shows an unusual sofa with tambour ends, a Seymour table under the banjo clock and a table hospitably set with old wineglasses, decanters and lotus pattern China Trade porcelain.

The dining room of the Asa Stebbins House is embellished with a Connecticut mahogany dining table inlaid with satinwood. The chairs are similarly inlaid, and are upholstered with yellow damask. A marble-top serving table stands at the right. The sideboard, by the celebrated Boston craftsman John Seymour, has frequently been illustrated in books on antique furniture. The tall case clock is an unusually small one made by Simon Willard.

The dining room sideboard, probably made by John Seymour about 1800, rather effects a union of the designs of Hepplewhite and Sheraton with its beautifully executed inlay, carving and reeding. The light and dark inlays on the tambour doors and the finely patterned crotch mahogany veneer also deserve special attention. Typical of Seymour are the ivory inlaid keyholes.

One of the exciting features of the work in connection with the preservation of the Asa Stebbins House was the discovery in several places of evidence of free-hand wall decoration. The red, black and green colors stood out with a refreshing quality on the yellow background. Certain portions of the original painting were carefully preserved and the balance was restored with the feeling of the original gaiety. Research has disclosed that these and other walls of the house were painted by Jared Jessup, a well known itinerant artist of the Connecticut Valley.

One is quite overcome by the number of fine pieces of China Trade porcelain, including a few Stebbins family pieces, in the dining room, most of them decorated with brilliantly colorful *famille rose* patterns.

Visible on one shelf in the pantry is a set of Lambeth Delft plates decorated in blue. Each arabesque or cartouche encloses part of a total story: "What is a merrey man . . . let him doe what he cane . . . to entertaine his guests . . . with wine and merrey jests . . . but if his wife doth frowne . . . all merriment goes downe."

The Jared Jessup free-hand designs also appear in the pantry, where a happy combination of blue and red border enlivens this attractive setting for shelves laden with glassware, plates, tureens and other colorful pieces. Many were made in China for the occidental market, while others are Delftware of either English or Dutch derivation.

The swag-type paper hangings in this bedroom must have been known in the area, for they were advertised in Greenfield newspapers from 1792 to the 1800's. The draperies carry the spirit of the paper both in color and design. The Connecticut bed has posts painted in delicate floral designs. The chairs and couch to the left are covered with a gay green silk bourette. The small chairs are painted black with gold decorations.

The Federal period dressing table is furnished with materials of the same time a delicate Trapunto cover and a plain cotton skirt. These semicircular dressing tables were advertised locally.

The swag drapes were fashioned to carry the color and design of this French wallpaper around the room, as shown here in the north bedroom. The "Captain Cook's Voyages" paper is seen in the hall. The Aubusson bedroom rug of red hues and the green-painted bed with delicate embroidered silk valence form an exquisite composition.

The paper in the south bedroom (opposite) and that in the hall (right) were brought from France by our then Ambassador, the Honorable James Bowdoin (for whom Bowdoin College is named) in the early years of the nineteenth century. They were placed in his friend Ruel Williams' mansion in Augusta, Maine. When this house was torn down a few years ago to make way for new highway work, the wallpapers were acquired and now adorn the walls of the Asa Stebbins house. They were designed by J. C. Charvet and made by DuFour in Macon, France, in 1804. One of the two known copies of the original old book of instructions for application and the detailed story of the individual panels in the "Captain Cook's Voyages" paper are owned by the Heritage Foundation. The complete set of twenty-one panels, plus a few repeats, can be seen in this house.

What more relaxing experience does a man (or woman) need, following a day on the road or touring museum houses, than to have a hearty meal at the DEERFIELD INN and to sit before a warming fire munching apples before retiring to soft, comfortable beds?

The PRATT HOUSE, for many years the residence of the town postmistress and keeper of a small store, is faced with wide, overlapping boards. Connected with it is a little shop displaying the tools of the broom-maker's trade, a thriving industry carried on in this area in the early days.

A school, a post office and a good hospitable inn are minimum essentials for a perfect New England village. Deerfield has all three. The shining white columns of its Deerfield Inn have welcomed, among others, generations of visiting parents, alumni and friends of Deerfield's three schools, and the Heritage Foundation preservation project.

Old Deerfield does not remain static in this century of its renaissance. Changes occur constantly as they do in other American communities, but here the transformation does not involve ranch houses, gas stations or supermarkets. Some changes can be traced to the increasing needs of the Academy, others to the restoration of the venerable houses on the village street. A conspicuous newcomer is the small white building which now occupies a site adjoining the Old Brick Church. The design of this pleasant little edifice under the elms is inspired by the long vanished Third Meeting House in Deerfield which was built about 1696. Early sketches and descriptions have marked it with a most unusual steeple in which hung, according to legend, the "Bell of St. Regis," originally cast in a French foundry. The present "Meeting House" has been constructed in recent years and now serves as the village post office. It has proven to be an agreeable place where friends may gather, where local news is discussed, and where tidings of the town are forwarded to those who have the misfortune to be away. The old building of 1696 was one story higher than its white-clapboarded successor in the heart of the Deerfield community.

Hall Tavern

The village street has been enriched in recent years by the addition of a rambling structure that once stood along the stagecoach highway to the west in Charlemont, Massachusetts. This is the Hall Tavern, for years the home of Joel and Lucretia Hall, built shortly after the middle of the eighteenth century, though added to later. It was carefully dismantled and reassembled in one of the few gaps along "The Street," where it now serves as an information center and as a poignant reminder of the romance, courage and enterprise of the early Americans.

The Hall Tavern might be called a very long and unconventional salt-box. Its faded clapboards carry pastel reminders of the many coats of paint which once covered its surface.

A springtime view of the Hall Tavern reveals its two ells and a squad of chimneys. The tower of the Old Brick Church shimmers through the foliage in the background.

Joel Hall had the reputation of being a genial host, content to dispense hospitality and good cheer in the old barroom to the varied clientele which passed through the fortified village of Charlemont. Fort Taylor was located here, and it was a place of thrilling adventures and grim tragedies. Hall's tavern was a resting place for drovers, teamsters and others of a hardy nature who sought good food, strong drink and a night's rest after a rough day along the highway. Lucretia Hall, the tavern-keeper's wife, did her full share to make the tavern a success. Her ability to cope with the brick oven and to bring forth fine early American dishes from the kitchen fireplace was as much a factor as her husband's good cheer. But she also found time to undertake the spinning, weaving, dyeing and sewing which were expected of a frontier housewife. The Halls took possession of this old place, presumably built in 1760, toward the end of the eighteenth century. By 1807 they were obliged to enlarge it and build a wing which contained a long, low shed above which was a ballroom with a vaulted ceiling. Many of the timbers in this new addition were transported from the dismantled Fort Taylor with the help of the neighbors.

Our modern insistence on creature comforts makes it difficult to understand how these roadside taverns could accommodate the large number of guests reported in historical accounts. The host's hospitality and the good cheer found at the bar perhaps made the guests less conscious of their discomfort. But Lucretia Hall provided for emergencies by laying aside woven bedspreads, blankets and ticks which could be filled with straw and spread on the ballroom floor. Many travelers brought their saddles, harness and blankets indoors with them, fearful that these cherished belongings might disappear during the night.

Nearly every Colonial village had its pewter shop, so it seems logical to find a collection of fine old pewter pieces in the Hall Tavern. Many of them are by Samuel Pierce, the celebrated pewterer from Greenfield, Massachusetts. The little silhouettes are in pewter frames possibly made by him.

98

A reasonable facsimile of Samuel Pierce, pewterer of nearby Greenfield, complete with corncob pipe, is installed before a reproduction of an old forge in the Hall Tavern. Samuel Pierce's original tools and molds are also on display, thanks to the generous gift of Ledlie Laughlin, author of *Pewter in America*.

A detailed view of some of Pierce's implements of the pewterer's craft includes his touchmark, believed to be the only known tool of this kind in America.

A long table set for the hungry traveler occupies the center of the tavern dining room. It is set with "treen" (wooden dishes), horn spoons and cups, some of imposing dimensions. The table also holds a collection of kitchen implements, a mechanical apple-peeler, and if further proof of Yankee ingenuity were needed, there is a fascinating corn-shucker in one corner, contrived of wooden wheels.

The oak court cupboard of the late seventeenth century is a Massachusetts piece which bears the original crest of the Saltonstall family. The chargers on the cupboard are Delft, depicting William and Mary of England.

At the rear of the tavern were the workroom and family quarters of the Halls. Here a commodious fireplace was equipped to prepare good food for the growing family and numerous guests. Against the pine wall is a spice chest from the Revere family and a cupboard for the host's clothes.

The parlor of the Hall Tavern has been furnished with old New England pieces, capturing much of the charm of the early days when it offered a refuge to feminine travelers while their men made merry in the barroom. The painted graining on the hall door shows up clearly at the left.

In the corner is a "poor man's court cupboard" of red painted pine. The curtains are French toile with the maker's mark imprinted on the edge.

This bedroom in the Hall Tavern has a structural feature not unusual for Deerfield: bricks are laid horizontally between the studs of the outside walls. The bed hangings and spread on the old four-poster are made from a printed linen with scenes depicting Penn's Treaty with the Indians.

The bedroom fireplace is framed with a natural wood molding which harmonizes with the wide sheathing.

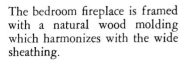

The "supper room" displays a large hutch table surrounded by Windsor chairs. The punch bowl, cover and plate are marked Wedgwood. Four cupboards are concealed in the simple sheathed wall. The stenciled borders on the yellow painted wall are based on a green oak-leaf and geometric design.

The ballroom is a low room of pleasing proportions with a vaulted ceiling and a floor of wide pine boards. The stiff wooden seats along the sides made the lot of the wallflower a hard one. To the right of the door is an area of the original stenciled plaster as it existed in Charlemont.

The ballroom of the Hall Tavern was heated by a single fireplace, which may seem hardly adequate for a cold winter night, but then country square dancers furnish their own warmth. The stenciling on fireplace and walls has been accurately reproduced from the designs of the original anonymous artist.

Old Manse

The story of this house is a full one. When the drawing took place among the pioneer settlers from Dedham, one of the most desirable lots, on a gentle knoll, fell to Nathaniel Colburne. This was in 1671. Two years later he sold the land to Joseph Gillet. Later both men were killed with Captain Lothrop's unfortunate company at Bloody Brook. Gillet's son sold the lot "with the house on it" to Samuel Carter in 1694. This might seem to establish the date of the gambrel-roofed cottage, which now serves as an ell. The Carter family was a large one. They lived here until the fateful night in 1704, when the Indians swooped over the stockade, murdering Mrs. Carter and some of the children, and leading the others away to captivity in Canada. Only the bereaved Samuel Carter remained behind in the house. One of the children returned from captivity, redeemed by means of "£24 borrowed money." One of the others married an Indian in Canada and refused to come back, and another married a French-Canadian girl. The disconsolate Carter sold the house to Samuel Allen and moved to Connecticut. In this way the house came into the family of the fiery Colonel Ethan Allen, the grandson of Samuel, although the leader of the Green Mountain Boys never actually owned it. The third Samuel to own the property was a wealthy merchant of Salem, Massachusetts, Samuel Barnard. In his will he bequeathed, besides considerable Salem property and family silver, this old property to his nephew, Joseph Barnard. The history of the Old Manse as one sees it today begins with this man of good taste, and the means to gratify it. He built this double hip-roofed house about 1768. The paneling is beautifully grained and free from knots. The Eastern Massachusetts influence is evident everywhere—wooden quoins, yellow-painted clapboards and graceful pilastered doorways, one on each side. But there is no rigid symmetry in the south façade, which is a masterpiece of subtle off-center spacing. The joiner, Jonas Locke, was from the Concord, Massachusetts, area. The house is supposed to have cost about a thousand pre-Revolutionary pounds, a figure which cannot easily be translated into contemporary dollars.

The Old Manse occupies a proud place on "The Street," directly opposite the Brick Church. Each of its four doorways follows a different design. Its fine double hip roof is contrived so that all of the rafters meet in the center, where a perpendicular rooftree holds them in place. Jonathan A. Saxton, a contributor to antislavery pamphlets, lived in the Old Manse in the nineteenth century, and there is a legend that it served as one of the stops on the "underground railroad." There was supposed to be a secret hiding place in the attic where runaway slaves could cling to an iron bar suspended high between the chimneys. A recent restoration, however, produced no evidence to substantiate this story. The Old Manse is now the property of Deerfield Academy.

The surviving timbers of the cottage inhabited by the martyred Carter family are now found in this gambrel-roofed wing. It has undergone many a change since 1694.

The northwest room in the Old Manse is now furnished as a dignified tea or game room. Back in 1792 it served a much more extraordinary purpose—the setting for a triple wedding, involving Joseph Barnard's granddaughters. By 1773 Barnard's son, Samuel, was living in the house. Known throughout the countryside as "Lawyer Sam," he was a Representative in the General Court. He and his wife, Abigail, had nine children, all born in the Manse. Much later they produced the greatest excitement the village had known for years, when three of their daughters married three young men from nearby Greenfield in the front parlor of their birthplace. All three of them—Nabby, aged 21, Rachel, 20, and Sally, a mere 18—were bedecked in identical sky-blue silk gowns on that Sunday morning in December, 1792. Joshua Clapp, Hart Leavitt and Dr. John Stone were the respective bridegrooms. Here was a theme for the local poets, and not a grim one. They made good use of it. Two years after this wedding "Lawyer Sam" sold the house to Ebenezer Williams, great-grandson of the pioneer, the Reverend John Williams. Its next distinguished tenant was Hosea Hildreth, a preceptor at Deerfield Academy. His son, the historian and diplomat, Richard Hildreth, author of a *History of the United States*, was born in the Old Manse.

When the Reverend Samuel Willard accepted the pastorate of Deerfield Parish in 1807, he first leased the Old Manse and then bought it for the precise sum of $3,333. The following May the young minister was married in Hingham. He drove his bride straight to Deerfield by chaise, a trip requiring four days. Her first appearance in church "wearing a fawn-colored silk spencer and white skirt, and a Leghorn hat trimmed with white" created a most favorable impression. People spoke of her lovely, graceful figure, her charming innocence of expression, her modesty and sweetness. To top all of these virtues, the pastor's new wife was musical. A pianoforte was installed in the Manse. It was a Clementi, and for years was the only one in the village. On pleasant summer evenings a group of villagers would gather in front of the house to hear Mrs. Willard play. The piano can still be seen in Memorial Hall. Dr. Willard loved music, too, and published a book of hymns he had written. Soon the Old Manse became the center of village life and more, as philosophers and statesman came as frequent guests. Francis Parkman, Horace Greeley, Dr. Channing and Ralph Waldo Emerson, who stayed a week, were a few of them. The respected minister began to lose his eyesight at forty-three and finally had to retire at the age of fifty-three. In 1885 his heirs sold the house. It fell into kind hands and today is in a remarkably good state of preservation.

The front hallway of the Old Manse is graced with a stair rail and an elaborately carved newel post which show the Salem influence strongly. The door, fashioned from two wide pine boards, is supported by extremely long strap hinges, part of the original hardware. Above it are five original panes of bull's-eye glass.

The mezzotint over the walnut veneer lowboy in the north parlor of the Old Manse is of Lord Jeffrey Amherst, after a portrait by Sir Joshua Reynolds. The table between the two windows is English, as is the settee next to the tea table.

The painstaking selection of perfectly grained and unblemished pieces of wood for the paneling would seem to indicate no intention of painting it. The wide pine panel over the fireplace is especially noteworthy. The rug is an early nineteenth-century Indian Agra of Pahamir design.

The carefully chosen woodwork in Joseph Barnard's southwest parlor remained in its natural state for many years before submitting to a coat of paint. Proof of this was furnished recently when the paint was removed, revealing six rectangles of lighter tone caused by six pictures which once hung over the fireplace.

The southeast room has a rare early wallpaper, a white background with colorful vines and flowers and a gaily colored bird. The rug is a late eighteenth-century Indian Agra.

On a wooded hill east of Deerfield village is a picturesque boarding school for boys ranging in age from six to fifteen. EAGLEBROOK SCHOOL accommodates 130 pupils and was founded in 1921 by Howard B. Gibbs. Perhaps its most pleasing structure is the headmaster's house. Thurston Chase is now headmaster.

Brick Church

The handsome, well-proportioned church which faces "The Street" at the north end of the Common is the fifth meeting house to be built in the village. Traces of the others have mostly disappeared. We know that the first was built before 1675 and that Samuel Mather was its minister. The third meeting house was built on the Common northwest of the Soldier's Monument and the fourth was erected on the Common where the Monument now stands in 1729. The serene structure which is veiled in elms today was built in 1824 for a blind minister, Samuel Willard. Funds for its construction were raised by public subscription. The land was bought for $530; the contributors to the fund were forty men and one woman—a most deceptive criterion of the godliness of Deerfield's housewives.

Recent research in local newspapers revealed that one Winthrop Clapp was the builder and designer in charge. The influence of Isaac Damon of New Haven, Connecticut, is clearly apparent as well as that of Asher Benjamin, a Greenfield man who gained considerable distinction because of his architectural and building books and whose design is seen in many houses and buildings in the area.

113

The interior of the Brick Church is chaste in its simplicity, ample in its seating accommodations. Each Sunday during the school term, boys at the Academy occupy its closed pews at the usual morning service for the townspeople. The service is now nonsectarian. The interior was restored in 1916.

The mahogany pulpit seems high now, but at one time it was even higher— on a level with the gallery. It has been stated that Isaac Damon built the original pulpit.

The Common is formed by a bulge about midway along Deerfield's wooded Street. Pillars of learning appear at this point, for the dominant buildings of Deerfield Academy face the Common. Between the sunny porch of the Ephraim Williams house in the foreground and the distant Brick Church is a lozenge-shaped parcel of lawn, dominated by two enormous sycamores. At one time an old store, run by a great Connecticut Valley merchant of the eighteenth century, Major Elijah Williams, was set between these aged trees. This store continued to prosper well into the nineteenth century under the Ware family. The Common has a touch of perpetual youth about it, despite such arboreal veterans. School-boys cross it frequently in droves, often on the run to get to class before the bell rings.

The Civil War Monument, cut in red stone, stands in the Common on the site of the vanished Fourth Meeting House. This monument designed by J. G. Batterson in 1867 is one of the largest built at the time.

A Salem, Massachusetts minister, the Reverend William Bentley, noted in his diary of 1788 some impressions of a visit to the village:

"Deerfield is three miles from the Connecticut, & the river upon which it lays empties into the Connecticut North of the Street, passing it upon the West. The interval land is excellent & overflowed in the Spring & Fall. The Street is one measured mile, running north & South, higher towards the South, & insulated in the common floods or freshets. The elevation is not gradual, but rather sudden north of the Meeting House, which stands on the west side, has an handsome appearance, electric rods, a public clock with pointers, & a good Bell. The rods are directed without the wain, from an ignorance of the electric principles. The School is on the open square in which the church stands & on the side of it is the Burying ground. Back stands an elegant House belonging to Mr. Williams. There is a gate at each end of the Street, & about 60 houses in the Street in better style, than in any of the Towns I saw. Several gentlemen liberally educated in the County reside here, & of the learned professions, but a distinguished opposition was here made to the american revolution, which required the interposition of the government, & the imprisonment of J. Williams, J. Ashley & Lieu: Carlton Esqrs. The resolution of the Government upon their proceedings is singular, & shews the evidence of the factions then prevailing."

Along that street one finds that the elevation north of the Meeting House has been made more gradual today by modern road construction. The successor to the Meeting House he saw is on the north side with a good bell, even though it has no public clock nor electric rods. A school (Deerfield Academy) is on the open square and the Burying Ground reposes serenely at the end of the road beside it. Back stands the elegant house of Mr. Williams. Alas, there are no gates at each end of "The Street." However, neither are there, even in this modern day, neon lights, garish store windows or cinemas. Of the sixty houses the Reverend Mr. Bentley noted as being "in better style than in any of the Towns" he saw, twenty-five still stand on their original foundations, as well as another fifteen that were erected shortly after his visit. Three which were built before his visit have been moved in since. If we add the present church, the post office, the Academy buildings, the reproduction of the "Indian House" (originally the Sheldon House, then the Hoyt Tavern), the grand total is fifty-three, compared to the 1788 count of sixty mentioned by the Reverend Mr. Bentley. The houses, open to visitors, contain over one hundred rooms and exhibitions, yet all have space to contain a private apartment as well. Thus the result is not a dead "museum village" nor a ghost town, but a vibrant and active community where people live and work.

Deerfield Academy

One of the finest preparatory schools in the United States faces the Deerfield Common. Its history is an imposing one. On March 21, 1797, Samuel Adams, then Governor of the Commonwealth, signed the Charter of Deerfield Academy. It was to be founded for "the promotion of piety, religion and morality, and for the education of youth in the liberal arts and sciences, and all other useful learning." The trustees held their first meeting on April 18, 1797, in the ballroom of the Frary House and voted to erect a brick building. The original minute book is still among the archives of the Academy. When the contemporary trustees assembled in the same room on April 18, 1947, just 150 years later, the minutes of this first meeting were read. The Academy formally opened its doors on January 1, 1799. Its first build-ing was a two-story structure which still flourishes as Memorial Hall. Asher Benjamin, author of that early American bible of building (first published in nearby Greenfield in 1797), *The Country Builder's Assistant,* was the architect. The story of the growth, decline and present enviable academic position of this New England Academy is an inspiring one which demands an entire book by itself. Anyone who knows Frank L. Boyden, headmaster since 1902, and his wife, Helen Childs Boyden, herself a native of Deerfield, can appreciate the reason for its present popularity, not only with its students but with parents, alumni and the entire world of education. "Be worthy of your heritage" is the motto of the Academy. There is abundant evidence that it has lived up to the aspirations of its founders.

The Recitation Building faces the Common and its ancient sycamores. Here is a "browsing" library and the wide-open hall which is the daily academic crossroads for students and faculty. Adjoining is the Science Building. These Georgian structures were designed by the late Charles A. Platt and erected in the 1930's. Three modern fireproof dormitories with eighteenth-century exteriors face the Common. They are located between the Manse and the Frary House, two venerable eighteenth-century masterpieces. Looking south, they are known as "Mather," "Scaife" and "Pocumtuck."

The Dining Hall, focal point thrice daily for hungry schoolboys, is a commodious structure which remains in the background. It was designed by William and Geoffrey Platt, sons of architect Charles A. Platt, and built in 1949.

The Infirmary, a brick structure based on the design of a house in Charlestown, New Hampshire, fits unobtrusively into the village scene. Built in 1949 and designed by the same architects, it accommodates fifty patients.

"The LITTLE BROWN HOUSE ON ALBANY ROAD," built about 1765, is an aged, unpainted cottage which first sheltered a shoemaker, then a wig-maker during the days of the Revolution. Towering over it for centuries before the ravages of the elm tree disease forced its elimination, was an immense elm which was considered by tree experts to be over three centuries old and the most ancient elm in the village. Its spacious branches once held a particular appeal to two contemplative citizens. One of them was General Epaphras Hoyt, who once owned the little brown house and lived there with his wife, Experience, known in the village as "Aunt Spiddy." Hoyt was a gifted man, a writer on military matters and the author of

Antiquarian Researches. The other citizen was Edward Hitchcock, a studious young man who later became a foremost geologist and rose to the Presidency of Amherst College. Between the two of them they built a refuge high in the branches where they could pursue their learned discussions free from the interruptions of their womenfolk.

A Connecticut Valley salt-box dwelling, The HITCHCOCK HOUSE, is another of the Academy buildings facing Albany Road. Elizabeth Amsden, a weaver, lived on the site in 1760. In 1778 John Williams sold it to Justin Hitchcock, a hatter, for 115 bushels of wheat. Justin was a fifer in Captain Locke's regiment which marched to Lexington. He also served under Colonel Joseph Stebbins in 1777. The house was inherited by his son, Henry, who was a saddler, and later by Nathaniel, a farmer. The other son, Edward, had loftier aspirations, as seen in the preceding paragraph.

John Williams House

A faded, parchment-covered folio recounts that in the year 1686 "The Inhabitants of Deerfield, to Incourage Mr. John Williams to settle amongst them to dispenc the blessed word of Truth unto them made propositions unto him as followeth: That they will give him 16 cowcommons of meadow land, with a home lott that lieth on the Meeting house hill. That they will build him a house: 42 foot long, 20 foot wide, with a leanto of the back side of the house, & finish sd house; to fence his home lott, and within two years after this agreement, to build him a barn, and to break up his plowing land." The "Inhabitants" who thus thirsted for spiritual leadership were the brave few who had returned to their ravaged lands after the devastation of King Philip's War and the handful of adventurers who were induced to join them. John Williams accepted and became the first resident minister of Deerfield. His house was erected at the time of his settlement in 1686 and there he lived for sixteen eventful years. Then came the fateful morning of February 28–29, 1704, and the historic raid. The Indians attacked his house, burned it and murdered two of his children and a Negro servant on the doorstone. The rest of the family was led through the snows to Canada. Eunice Williams, the parson's wife, perished in the early days of the march. All of the others were eventually redeemed except little Eunice, her mother's namesake. She was adopted and baptized by Chris-

tian Indians, later married one of them, had a son and two daughters, and lived to be close to ninety. John Williams' days in captivity were not wasted. He observed enough during his tormented travels to be able to write, in later years, *The Redeemed Captive,* the accepted American classic on the subject. After he returned to Boston from his Canadian captivity, it was not long before a committee of Deerfield citizens persuaded him to return to his flock. At a town meeting in January, 1706, it was voted to build him a new house "as big as Ens. John Sheldon's." This was accomplished in 1707. Legend has it that the ghost of Eunice Williams still wails mournfully through the property, particularly on bitterly cold nights.

The John Williams property and other houses on the Common stood near the side of the highway which had been marked out in the early town records to run "westerlie" into the meadows "as may best accommodate the meadows and the fesibleness of the passage into the same." This highway has been known for generations as the Albany Road.

In 1754 surveyors further defined the road and it became more frequently used by travelers to the west. It was to Deerfield that people seemed to look for supplies, news and social events. By 1762 Major Elijah Williams, son of the Reverend John Williams and successful merchant, had erected the house we see today (on land along the Common inherited from his father) and a general store which was patronized by the people of Deerfield and neighboring towns. The elegantly proportioned front door-frame with its broken pediment and scroll was fashioned by a joiner from Hatfield in the 1750's. Local joiners carved the splendid interior paneling and undoubtedly the window headers and side door with its less elaborate but refined frame. The house as we see it today lends charm and elegance to the old John Williams property. In 1789 the house was sold to Consider Dickinson, a staunch New England farmer, hunter, fur-trader and soldier. Known locally as "Uncle Sid," his fund of humorous anecdotes and songs was apparently limitless. In 1875 it was willed to Deerfield Academy and is now cherished as the Academy's most historic building. It serves as a dormitory for younger boys.

The EPHRAIM WILLIAMS HOUSE, just south of the Common, was built in 1760 by John Partridge Bull, armorer to Colonel Williams' regiment. The Colonel's nephew, Dr. William Stoddard Williams, and his descendants lived in this house from the 1790's to the early days of this century. Dr. Williams also had his office here. For years this has been the residence of "The Head," Mr. Frank L. Boyden, and Mrs. Boyden. It has long been the heart of Deerfield Academy. The rising fortunes of the school during the past half-century are clearly attributable to them.

In 1759 the town petitioned the General Court for permission to sell to tradesmen the lots sequestered for the use of the Ministry along the south side of the Albany Road, because "the soil of sd. lot is poor and Baren & for want of manure is rendered of but little proffit to the Minister." About 1760 David Saxton erected this house at the corner, which he operated as a tavern. During the hectic Revolutionary War days it was known as a Whig tavern. It is now known as the SAXTON HOUSE. Although not open to the public, it should be noted that the front hall reveals evidence of early exotic wall paintings. Also, the early tavern ballroom lines are still distinguishable, even though greatly changed by the demands of modern living.

The HINSDALE-WHITING HOUSE, sometimes called the Harrow House, is of ample proportions. It is a veteran of the eighteenth century, but was remodeled extensively about 1806 by William Russell.

Frary House

This ancient house facing the south end of the Common, is associated with the very dawn of this frontier settlement. Part of it was built by Samson Frary, son of one of the original Dedham proprietors, somewhere in the 1680's. Historians are not in agreement on the date of the early north part of the house, which may be 1683. Parts of this section of the house, together with parts of the gambrel-roofed ell of the Manse and perhaps a portion of the Nims House and some other houses are all that remain of the valiant seventeenth-century frontier village. The Frary House escaped the tragic fire and massacre of 1704, but its owners did not. Samson Frary was murdered and his wife was killed during the march to Canada.

Many decades later, in 1763, Major Selah Barnard bought the house for 175 pounds. A former military man, he had peaceful leanings. They tell a pleasant story of his marriage. Back in 1746 when he was leaving home for the wars, he dropped in at a neighbor's house to say good-bye. He saw a baby lying in its cradle and said to its mother, "Keep her until the wars are over and I will marry her." Just twenty years later Miss Elizabeth Nims, the infant of 1746, became the wife of the Major turned inn-keeper, in a pretty ceremony in the old Frary House. Barnard evidently prospered as a landlord, for he built the southern addition with the ballroom in 1768. During the Revolutionary War Barnard's Tavern became the gathering place of the Whigs and a natural stopover for sympathizers of the patriots' cause. When Benedict Arnold, bedecked in a shining new Colonel's uniform, came to Deerfield in May, 1775, he put up at the tavern. His mission was to buy 15,000 pounds of beef for the army then forming. He sent for a leading citizen, Thomas W. Dickinson, and sealed a bargain for the beef, according to tradition, in landlord Barnard's taproom. From there the ambitious Arnold hurried into Vermont enroute to Ticonderoga, where he hoped to enhance his reputation at the expense of the British—but he was too late. Fort Ticonderoga had surrendered to the fiery Ethan Allen, grandson of a Deerfield citizen, and his Green Mountain Boys. Arnold went on to fame at Quebec and Saratoga, and final disgrace at West Point.

Selah Barnard's son, Erastus, later inherited the tavern and was the landlord when the trustees of the newly formed Deerfield Academy held their first meeting in the ballroom in 1797. In those pre-dormitory days the tavern occasionally sheltered unusual students of the Academy. In the early 1800's the heir apparent to the throne of the Sandwich Islands, Cryamakoo, lived here under the assumed name of John Meek and went dutifully to classes.

The ensuing years were not kind to the house. It passed through many hands and varied forms of neglect. Toward the end of the century its roof leaked badly and the lean-to leaned too much. Hens roosted in the entry way and there were no windows in the parlor, a room then used for sorting tobacco. Circus posters covered the space where the front door had been when Miss C. Alice Baker, a descendant of the original John Frary, bought the house in 1890. A person of vision and courage, she preserved it from destruction and willed it to the Pocumtuck Valley Memorial Association. It has been faithfully restored in the spirit of Colonial times.

The unpainted south doorway of the Frary House is delicately carved and browned with age.

The taproom which occupied the sunny southwest corner of Selah Barnard's tavern was cheerful and ele-mental, for it was used for convivial gatherings. Tankards and pipes, game boards and candles were all put to use as men gathered near the warm fire. Cartoons of the day were posted on the walls for everyone's enjoyment.

It isn't difficult to imagine the proud and famous Colonel Benedict Arnold seated with a toddy at the table in this taproom and putting through an urgent cattle deal with the local beef baron. Happily, this took place before the Colonel became infamous.

A room furnished as the tavern keeper's office or workroom brings to the house a feeling that the tavern was really lived in.

The bar in the Barnard Tavern (Frary House) is small, yet practical. Its Dutch door could be locked at night. Another door led to the tavern keeper's office. The door shown behind the counter, under the shelves, led to the cellar where casks and containers were stored. The framed document on the door is the original license issued by the Selectmen to Nathan Frary, authorizing the sale of spirituous liquors in 1752.

The parlor of the Frary House contains Augustus Tack's portrait of Miss C. Alice Baker, the far-sighted descendant of Samson Frary, who rescued the house from virtual oblivion in 1890. Her kindly and vivid personality is still felt throughout the house.

Layers of paint were scraped from the woodwork of the Blue Room to find the shade of powder blue which now gives the room its subtle glow. The fireplace is spanned by an immense stone lintel and framed in wide panels. Other walls are covered with a copy of an old Deerfield paper.

The old kitchen of the Frary House has been restored to its pioneer aspect, down to the vital musket over the fireplace. Early records show that a buttery, with ladder-like stairs leading to the loft, existed on one side of the old kitchen. On the other side was a "borning-room," equipped with a bed and so placed that it caused the young mother the least in convenience in preparing her meals. Both of these early refinements have been restored.

Over the centuries this room has served many purposes—a store, a kitchen and a dining room, its present function. The table and sideboard display some of Miss Baker's best pewter.

At the far end of the southern ell is the "summer kitchen" of the Frary House. Its broad fireplace was well fitted to handle the cooking for Selah Barnard's warm-weather guests.

The ballroom of the Frary House is light and airy, the most festive room in Deerfield, which is as it should be. This is a fiddler's view of the room, taken from the small gallery into which the musicians were crowded. They had the best view of the fine old chandeliers and the dance floor too. This addition, the south wing, was probably built by landlord Selah Barnard in 1768 and served as a gathering place for Deerfield Whigs in the formative days of the Republic. In later years its mission was more carefree. Dances, plays and concerts were held in its cheerful confines. More important, the cause of education took fertile root in this room on April 18, 1797, when the Board of Trustees of Deerfield Academy held their first meeting.

The ballroom fireplace (right) is flanked by two arched recesses, discreet refuges where the Colonial lass could sit out a dance with her partner. The delicate rope molding and reeded decoration which appear throughout the room are discernible in this view.

The gallery for the musicians is coquettish, enclosed with a delicate railing. It is entered by a ladder from an adjoining card room. Equally refined are the doorway, the vaulted ceiling and paneled side benches, uncompromisingly hard as they' are. But more than this is needed to create a vivid picture of the ballroom as it looked in Colonial days. It takes a starry evening, pretty girls in tight bodices and full skirts, handsome village blades . . . and a minuet.

The upstairs chambers of the Frary House aroused no compassion for the weary traveler in Selah Barnard's time. Indications are that the rooms were as cheerful, ample and clean as, for example, the north chamber is today.

The NIMS HOUSE, a broad gambrel-roofed structure, adjoins the Frary House on the south, and is almost as venerable. The homestead dates back to Godfrey Nims, one of Deerfield's earliest and most turbulent settlers. His first house was burned by the Indians in 1704, three of his little daughters perishing in it. Two other children were killed, his wife died on the march, and two children trudged into captivity and a new life in Canada. Strange and romantic stories are told of them and their descendants. The present house was built about 1710 and now belongs to the Academy. At one time it was the headquarters of the Blue and White Embroidery Society.

The TOWN HALL (1846), a more recent Greek revival addition to the Deerfield scene, is one of the most harmonious. Its white Ionic columns and graceful pediment show up particularly well in the reflected light of a sunny morning following a fall of snow. The village library is located here. Its most popular use is for town meetings and theatrical performances.

The little WHITE CHURCH on Memorial Street was built in 1837 at the difficult moment when New England churches split on the issue of Unitarianism. In the background is a fine Colonial house once lived in by John Wilson and now owned by the Academy.

Memorial Hall

The dignified building which Asher Benjamin designed for Deerfield Academy was abandoned for more commodious school quarters long ago, but its educational destiny has never changed. In 1878 it was considerably altered to become the headquarters and museum of the newly formed Pocumtuck Valley Memorial Association. The venerable white-bearded George Sheldon and a group of Deerfield citizens established this historical society to "illustrate and perpetuate the history of the early settlers," and named the old brick building Memorial Hall, in recognition of these pioneers and their heroic struggle for existence.

The Association has assembled, in this transformed academy, a truly extraordinary collection of furniture, china, glass, pictures, costumes and a multitude of other evidences of Colonial living. It has created a library containing such a wealth of books, diaries, letters and manuscripts that one may risk the statement that Deerfield is one of the best documented villages in New England.

Several rooms have been furnished to present an accurate picture of Colonial life—a kitchen, a parlor, a dining room, a bedroom, a schoolroom and a children's room. There are exhibits of spinning and weaving equipment, old fabrics and needlework, a collection of guns, and a remarkable group of Indian artifacts. Trade shops have been set up, showing the types of implements used by coopers, tanners, harness-makers and cobblers.

Memorial Hall is one of the most remarkable things in this remarkable village, a museum of greater attainment than one dares expect, even in Deerfield.

The original bell which summoned Deerfield Academy students to their classes has been brought inside, and now hangs over the schoolroom door. The teacher's desk and chair were used by John Wilson, village printer, when he became an Academy "steward." The writing on the blackboard (itself original) is a chalk copy of words, figures and chirography from early Deerfield schoolbooks.

Significant among the portraits in Memorial Hall is this crisp delineation of Elijah Arms of Deerfield, painted about 1800 by William Jennys, a notable artist of the primitive school.

One of the treasures of Memorial Hall is this beautiful old spinet, made in London shortly before 1685 by Stephanus Keene. Samuel Pepys once bought a similar one for five pounds. It is believed to be one of three of its kind in the world today. It was owned by Mrs. Willard, the minister's wife.

At the left in this large exhibition room is a corner cupboard from the John Williams house, filled with old Canton ware. The portrait is of a member of the Williams family. Beneath it is one of the first pianofortes to appear in Deerfield, the Clementi which belonged to Mrs. Susan Willard.

The portrait of the patriarch George Sheldon, founder of this remarkable museum, is by Augustus Tack. The Windsor comb-back writing chair is stamped by the maker, Tracy, and the desk is made of Santo Domingo mahogany. The chairs to the left are quite early.

The third floor of Memorial Hall is given over to a fascinating miscellany of old shop signs, bootmakers' equipment and relics of Deerfield's early industries.

A fine old loom is installed on the second floor, along with spinning and weaving equipment. At the left is a painted chest dating from the eighteenth century, one of a large collection owned by the Association.

The most vivid and moving reminder of the Massacre of 1704 has been preserved in Memorial Hall. It is the door from the original Sheldon House, known as the Old Indian House. A horseshoe is nailed ironically on the lintel. Below it is the heavy door, studded with nails and split in the middle by Indian tomahawks, similar to one which is imbedded in the wood.

Wells-Thorn House

This photograph, taken half a century ago, proved of invaluable assistance in this Deerfield restoration project. The house is an excellent complement to many of the others which, like it, have graced the village street for more than 200 years. This is one of the houses that the Reverend William Bentley must have seen. Its central section was constructed about 1717 in the seventeenth-century manner, while the main part was put on in 1751. The front doorway is of a later vintage.

The pioneer Ebenezer Wells was the original owner of the lot. He built himself a simple two-room "split level" house. Because of the slope of the land to the rear, the kitchen was several steps below the level of the "keeping room." When the Indian threats had passed and Ebenezer had become a well-to-do farmer, tavern-keeper and merchant, he added a front section in the mid-eighteenth century tradition. This was in 1751, and quite in keeping with the Deerfield house construction practice.

It was probably in 1783 that the Wells family further embellished it by adding decorative window caps. By 1801 the property had passed to Hezekiah Wright Strong, who made some interior changes. Still later the Ware family operated a livery stable here. During the first half of this century Dr. and Mrs. E. C. Thorn resided in the house.

This early spring picture of the Wells-Thorn House reveals the subtlety of the early buds, the soft yellow clapboards, the strong central chimney and the fine rough quality of the shingles that cover the roof. Research efforts have not yet been sufficiently conclusive regarding the exact design of the original front door.

The house as it is today presents a low shed-like appendage at the east end, as noted in the earlier picture. Sometime during the life of the house this appendage was added and used for varied purposes—a shop, store and even part of a livery stable, possibly the office and harness room. This section, however, was removed early in this century. Fortunately, the negative of the early photograph by the Allen sisters survived, so the wing was reconstructed from this evidence. It now encloses a modern two-bedroom apartment.

Natural wood of a soft rosy tone and off-white paint have been used in combination on the woodwork of the north parlor, redecorated by the lawyer, Hezekiah Wright Strong. Among the distinguished furnishings are an Eliphalet Chapin tall chest, desk-bookcase and chairs. The Chippendale sofa, the easy chair upholstered in gold damask, and a clock dated 1773 by Preserved Clapp of Amherst, Massachusetts, also show to advantage in this room.

One of Connecticut's foremost cabinet-makers, Eliphalet Chapin of East Windsor, moved to Hartford in 1783. This tall chest, a superb example of his type of work, was originally owned by Hezekiah Strong's cousin, Caleb Strong of Northampton, who was one of the first United States Senators from Massachusetts (1789) and was Governor of Massachusetts during 1800–1807 and again during 1812–1816. It is of cherry, with claw-and-ball feet. The broken scroll pediment is composed of two moldings terminating in typical whorls, with fret-carved trellis work that undoubtedly shows the influence of Chapin's residence in Philadelphia, where he worked under Savery, the great craftsman of that Colonial city. The corners of both sections are chamfered and have stop-fluting with capitals and bases adorned with bronze. Another piece (right) that belonged to Governor Caleb Strong is this desk-bookcase. Unlike the tall chest, the drawers are beaded and the feet are of the well-proportioned ogival bracket type. The pediment and fret-carved trellis work are also ornamented by three baluster-shaped finials on molded plinths.

The proportions of the south parlor of the Wells-Thorn house provide a splendid setting for some noteworthy furnishings. The Allis family chest-on-chest, revealing strong local character, has stood in this particular house for over half a century. It was acquired within a few miles of Deerfield, and is believed to have been the work of a local craftsman. The rug is a superb Kouba of the seventeenth century, with an unusually large geometric pattern in brilliant colors.

The original corner cupboard contains fine English ceramics, such as a pair of beautifully formed Whieldon deer, a two-handled Whieldon cup, some Astbury type pieces and numerous salt glaze plates and figures.

A few steps above the kitchen in the 1717 section of this house is the "keeping room," or, in an early English term, "the hall." It is furnished for general use by the family with seventeenth and eighteenth-century household items. The bed, chairs, tables and chests all depict the simple living of the locality at this period. The portraits are of Queen Anne, attributed to J. Cooper, and Prince George of Denmark, her spouse, by a later painter. The table rug is an Oushak, conceived in the Holbein pattern.

To the garret (below) were relegated out-of-fashion or outgrown objects, such as engravings of George III, a wooden cradle, old chairs and spinning wheels.

The south chamber on the second floor is sheathed in its original pine boards and contains a pencil post bed dressed in a simple but handsome style of the period, a serpentine front Chippendale chest with claw-and-ball feet, and a few articles of clothing of the period.

A discreet glimpse through the clerk's office on the second floor shows the large room beyond that was at one time Hezekiah Wright Strong's law office, with a door leading to the outside staircase. Visible are a chest of drawers and, on the right, a large bookcase that held the lawyer's books.

The façade of The BENJAMIN RAY HOUSE catches its full share of spring sunlight. Benjamin Ray, a carpenter and wagon-maker, built his house in 1835. His daughters helped him buy lumber for it by making baskets and braiding palm-leaf hats.

147

The TIMOTHY CHILDS HOUSE stands white and serene under its protecting elms. Captain Childs probably built the house in the first half of the eighteenth century and lived here for about thirty years. For years this was known as the Champney House, after Mr. and Mrs. J. Wells Champney, who lived here in the late nineteenth century. He was a well-known artist and the first art teacher at Smith College. The doorway which the Champneys added is an obvious appendage, but an interesting one. It was originally the entrance to Alexander Hamilton's home on Grove Street in New York.

The AUGUSTUS LYMAN HOUSE was erected in 1803 on the site of the ill-starred Nathaniel Brooks house, burned in 1704. It was purchased by Ephraim Williams and was the birthplace of his son, John Williams, later Bishop of Connecticut. It stands on the west side of the village street opposite Memorial Street which goes east to the state highway.

Dwight-Barnard House

One of only three "old newcomers" prominent on the village Street is a dignified gambrel-roofed house bearing the strong stamp of the Connecticut Valley. While it looks as though it had always been in Deerfield, it originally stood in Springfield where it was built, probably about 1754, by Josiah Dwight, a merchant with connections in many towns along the Connecticut River. He was a brother of Timothy Dwight, an early President of Yale. In 1950, when the old house was about to be demolished by wreckers, it was rescued and transported board by board to Deerfield. Its missing doorway has never been recovered, but an exact copy of the original has been substituted. The sturdy frame, fine brick chimney and handsome paneled rooms were largely intact. The house was painstakingly rebuilt on its new site, appropriately furnished with period pieces, and opened to the public in 1954. Many of the early furnishings in the house belonged to the Williams family of Deerfield. The Williamses were related to Josiah Dwight, builder of the house, and both families were related to the Flynt family, descendants of which in the present generation have preserved, restored and furnished the house.

A doctor's office has been established on the ground floor of the Dwight-Barnard House as a tribute to Dr. Thomas Williams and his son, Dr. William Stoddard Williams, who between them guarded the health of this community for almost a century. All the furniture, the scales and sundry other objects belonged to them. These objects are here because of the generous interest and help of Elizabeth Fuller of Deerfield, a trustee of the Heritage Foundation and herself a descendant of the Doctors Williams.

The atmosphere of an eighteenth-century working kitchen has been captured in this room in the Dwight-Barnard House. The floors are brick and the walls are covered with wide pine sheathing. At the left is a rare apothecary cabinet, painted a dark bluish green. Local pottery graces the early Connecticut dresser.

The large kitchen fireplace is a reproduction of one built in 1738 in New Salem, Massachusetts. Its massive oak lintel supports a heavy wooden lug pole. With oven and alcoves for kettles and bottles, it is highly utilitarian. Herbs of the same type as those grown by Dr. Williams hang from the rafters.

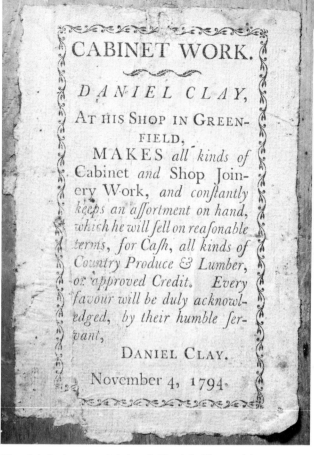

The pill slab hanging over the porringer top table is Delft with the seal of the Apothecaries' Guild bearing the words *Opiferque per orbem dicor* ("I am called a helper throughout the world"). The print depicts the death of General Wolfe. This and other prints in the room are similar to subjects owned by Dr. Thomas Williams.

The label (upper right) of Daniel Clay, cabinetmaker of Greenfield, is in the tall clock in the parlor.

This chest of drawers was given to Mary Hoyt by her father when she married Dr. William Stoddard Williams. Their portraits hang in the doctor's office.

The parlor of the Dwight-Barnard House reveals a more refined architectural treatment and more sophisticated furniture than the other rooms of the house. The tea set of China Trade porcelain rests on a table which belonged to the Williams family. The portrait of Dr. Joseph Trumbull is by Ralph Earl.

The vista of the parlor ends with a fine tall cherry clock which carries the label of Daniel Clay, Greenfield, dated 1794.

In one corner of the parlor is a superb mahogany bombé secretary of Boston origin, formerly owned by the Ames and Whitney families of that city. In this desk are many mementos of the Williams family, including a draft of a statement which Dr. Thomas Williams prepared for the Colonial treasurer claiming, as executor of the estate of his brother, Colonel Ephraim Williams, reimbursement for certain expenses he had incurred in connection with the Crown Point expedition. The doctor had accompanied him on this trip, but fared better than the Colonel, who was ambushed and killed there on September 7, 1755. On the way to Lake George, the Colonel had made a will at Albany, leaving a portion of his estate to found a school in the northwest township of the Commonwealth. This became Williams College. Deerfield's Parson Jonathan Ashley was successful in securing a charter, signed by the Colonial Governor, to have the school established east of the Berkshire Hills—if not actually in Deerfield, then in a township of Hampshire County. The Harvard Overseers feared the effect of another college so close to Cambridge, and thus had the legislative branch annul the Governor's grant and issue a new one locating the proposed institution west of the mountains, clearly the intention of the testator. Parson Ashley, knowing that the Colonel had resided in Deerfield (his father and brother are buried in the old graveyard) and supported by a map (doubtless similar to one now on his study door) argued that Deerfield was in the northwesterly township and was entitled to have the school located here. The parson, not too easily turned aside from his fixed purpose, hastened on horseback to Norwalk, Connecticut, with the hope that a victorious and popular British general might intercede. Not wishing to become involved in British Colonial politics, the general refused to cooperate. The general was none other than Lord Jeffrey Amherst, whose name was appropriated a half century later for a new college formed along the Connecticut River when the President and some of the Williams faculty defected from the college named for Colonel Williams.

The paneling in the south chamber is remarkable for its original rose-cedar graining, the coved cornice over the chimney breast and the curious design of the pilasters. In the large single panel hangs a needlework version of the "Reclining Shepherdess." Most of the chairs and the dressing table are Williams family pieces. In the same room is a Williams bed, dressed with colorful crewel work. Next to the window is the cradle in which the Williams children were rocked as infants. The table is an old Deerfield piece.

In the north chamber of the Dwight-Barnard House is a canopied bed, painted white, gold and green, made as a wedding present for the younger Dr. Williams. It has a crewel-work bedcover with the legend "Betsy Clark, her work 1767." A Martha Washington chair stands in the foreground. The rug is an Aubusson.

The hand-loomed linen spread was found in the town dump by Margaret Whiting and Ellen Miller, who founded the Deerfield Society of Blue and White Needlework in 1895. This detail of the border shows the fine use of simple stitches which, unlike those above, are worked in polychrome.

Strolling south in the fleeting beauty of a spring day, one approaches the Dwight-Barnard House (1754) on the west side of "The·Street," with the white clapboards of the Higginson-Childs House (1797) in the distance. Returning northward the vista is equally lovely in its tranquillity.

The HOYT HOUSE lends a touch of Federal refinement to the southern end of "The Street." It may be possible to discern here the graceful detail associated with Asher Benjamin, architect from nearby Greenfield. Twenty-six of his drawings were found on this property. This was the home of David Starr Hoyt, the engineer whose small party planted the United States flag on the summit of Popocatepetl during the Mexican War.

The JOSEPH BARNARD HOUSE is faced with unusual boards, grooved to present an even pattern. Five generations of the Barnard family have occupied this house since 1764. It now serves as a residence for an Academy master.

Wilson Printing House

Perhaps the most migratory of all Deerfield houses is this faded veteran which has come back to roost, after five moves, on the spot of its original foundation. It began its career as the print shop of John Wilson, who built the house in 1816 with the aid of his brother-in-law, Rodolphus Dickinson. Their wives were granddaughters of David Hoyt, landlord of the favorite Tory tavern during the Revolution. Both men had literary leanings. Wilson, who had been detained in Canada shortly before the War of 1812 on charges that he was an American spy, wrote such a brilliant defense that he secured his freedom. Dickinson was a more prolific writer. His numerous books dealt mostly with religion, geography and legal procedure. His most successful work was the *Compendium of the Bible*. This ran through six editions and was sold by book agents all through New England and in New York State. Rodolphus Dickinson left the partnership, but Wilson continued publishing until 1820. A man of unquestioned versatility, he became successively a steward of Deerfield Academy, civil engineer, inventor and manufacturer. The spirit of enterprise of this Deerfield man deserves particular recognition. In addition to the printing office, the building had room for a book bindery. The upper floor was obviously used for supplies. The second-story door and over it the beam with a pulley clearly indicate this use.

The "Customer's Room," cheerful and well lighted, offered a welcome retreat to the village literati. Over the fireplace hang paintings on glass representing the four continents.

A genuine eighteenth-century press is difficult to find. The pressroom of the Wilson Printing House is fitted with the next best thing, a careful copy of the original owned by Isaiah Thomas, the celebrated Colonial printer of Worcester. That rare early press is now owned by the American Antiquarian Society.

The Wilson Printing House began its travels in the 1820's when John Wilson apparently sold the entire building to grocer Catlin, who was also a cabinet-maker. It was moved across the street and served as Catlin's woodworking shop. At the next point in its career it became Hiram McKee's wagon shop near the Town Hall. Houses were shunted about easily in those days, especially small ones, and this one made two more moves, which have baffled the keen efforts of research experts, before settling down at its starting point. It has now been restored and fitted with the essentials of an early print shop, much as it appeared in Wilson's day.

The southern extremity of "The Street" is carpeted with leaves on an October morning. Its houses are varied . . . a Connecticut Valley farmhouse, a two-chimneyed printer's shop and a hip-roofed town house.

A Whittier is needed to do justice to the landscape which unfolds on every fringe of Deerfield. This snow-clad road is one of the few which lead from the village plateau to the river valley.

The present ABERCROMBIE HOUSE at the southern extremity of "The Street" gleams white behind its trim picket fence, framed in dense green foliage. A typical Connecticut Valley house, it was probably built by Eleazer Hawks in 1712. For years it was called the Farrington House, in memory of one of the Dedham proprietors.

Our stroll down Deerfield's wooded thoroughfare ends in a blaze of glory as "The Street's" southernmost maple bursts into autumn gold. Beyond, on a lower level, are the south meadows, the tobacco barns and the rich stretches of loam which lured the courageous settlers to this martyred outpost in the late 1600's.

The Front Door: John Williams House, *circa* 1754.

A Portfolio Of Old Deerfield Details

Front doorway of the Ashley House.
Adaptation of a doorway, *circa* 1750.

Front doorway of the Dwight-Barnard House.
Reproduction of the doorway, 1754.

Front doorway of the Allen House.
Adaptation of a doorway, *circa* 1750.

Front doorway of the Thomas Dickinson House,
circa 1752.

Side doorway of the John Williams House,
circa 1754.

Side doorway of the Joseph Stebbins House,
circa 1772.

Northern doorway of three on west side of the
Hall Tavern.
Adaptation of a doorway, *circa* 1760.

Front doorway of the Manse, *circa* 1768.

Front doorway of the Asa Stebbins House, 1799.

Front doorway of the Hinsdale House, 1806.

Front doorway of the Wells-Thorn House,
circa 1820.

Front doorway of the Wright House, 1824.

Connecticut Valley desk-bookcase in the
Allen House.

Seymour secretary with maker's label in the
Wright House.

Connecticut Valley tall chest in the Ashley House.

Elihu Ashley's tall chest in Memorial Hall.

Original label from the desk in the Chippendale Room of the Wright House (right) made by "Benj.n Frothingham Cabbinet Maker in Charlestown, N.E." The label was engraved by Nathaniel Hurd, whose initials appear beneath the cartouche.

This rare walnut veneer lowboy is of the Queen Anne style. It has a mariner's star inlay which appears on the sides and is matched and featured on the top. The extruded gilt shell has a sanded background and the carved and gilded apron pendants are original. Rare Spanish or Flemish scroll feet make this probably the best known of its type. It is a Massachusetts piece of about 1720–1730. It is in the south parlor, Sheldon-Hawks House.

Block-front mahogany slant lid desk by Frothingham, of Massachusetts origin with hairy claw-and-ball feet. The interior cabinet has a carved shell in the arched recess of the center door, blocked drawers and pigeonholes, and original Chippendale-type brasses. (From the Chippendale Room, Wright House.)

Light cherry lowboy or dressing table of the mid-eighteenth century. The top and sides are scalloped in a distinctive manner, and the central lower door has a simple sunburst. Square cabriole legs end in unusual pad feet that appear to be ribbed and notched; probably made in Deerfield or Hatfield, Massachusetts, by a local cabinet-maker. It is in the south chamber, Sheldon-Hawks House.

Shell-crowned cupboard in the north parlor of the Ashley House.

Pine corner cupboard in the kitchen of the Ashley House.

Shell-crowned cupboard in the parlor of the Dwight-Barnard House.

Cupboard in the Sheldon-Hawks House with Society of the Cincinnati porcelain mentioned on page 153

Detail of the Connecticut Valley tall chest, Ashley House.

EPILOGUE

When the question arises—as it often does—as to why we became interested in Deerfield, the answer is not hard to find. After long familiarity with the region and association with Deerfield Academy, we came to love this unique village. For a quarter of a century we have cherished our close, friendly relationship with Frank Boyden, the famous headmaster of Deerfield Academy, and his extraordinary wife, Helen Childs Boyden. We sensed an opportunity to help perpetuate the traditions and beauty of the village from an historical, educational and practical point of view. As academy housing problems became difficult, we realized that preserving some of the old houses could accomplish three things—provide better living for the faculty of Deerfield Academy, give some local employment and provide museums of historic significance.

As one strolls along this quiet, imposing street at any season of the year, even in the winter, as lights appear in hundreds of ancient windows and smoke curls from the large chimneys, the ineffable charm of Deerfield becomes manifest. Architecture, history, education and its courageous people have given Deerfield its distinction, a symbol of what is right in America. Many Deerfield residents proudly maintain their homes in order to preserve the spirit of the early days and to be worthy of their heritage.

The Indian House Association owns a replica of an early Sheldon home, the central point of the 1704 attack. As early as 1848 an attempt was made to save the original house and, though unsuccessful, it was one of the very early efforts to preserve an historic American building.

Deerfield Academy has long sought to preserve the character of the town. The records of the academy also show that in its early days a museum was established where artifacts of Deerfield's proud past, as well as natural phenomena and objects from foreign lands, were preserved for the benefit of students and visitors. Thus, at Deerfield a sig-

nificant step was taken in the museum world more than a century and a half ago.

The Pocumtuck Valley Memorial Association, through its collections, its ownership of the Memorial Hall Museum and the Frary House, has for many years been instrumental in perpetuating Deerfield's past.

Because of the energy and enthusiasm of George Sheldon (1818–1916), Deerfield's eminent historian, and his scholarly wife, Jenny Arms Sheldon, the Historical Society is the beneficiary of an amazing collection of Indian artifacts, Deerfield and Connecticut Valley documents, books and family memorabilia, as well as furniture, ceramics, fabrics and countless other items, depicting a way of life which otherwise might easily be forgotten or ignored.

Our generation and those to follow owe a heavy debt of gratitude also to the ladies of the village, not only those who were born here, but several who moved here at the beginning of this century. Their appreciation of the arts and crafts of the early settlers, of their needlework and embroidery, led to a practical revival of these evidences of their culture and taste.

Since 1942 Mrs. Flynt and I have given of our time, enthusiasm and resources to carry forward the "Deerfield Project" in a manner which we trust is dignified and correct and may continue to prove appealing. We hope to pursue this work indefatigably, yet we are conscious of the limitations of time. To insure perpetuity to our efforts, the Heritage Foundation was created in 1952. Among other things, the Charter, granted by the Commonwealth of Massachusetts, provides that it is "To promote the cause of education in and appreciation of the rich heritage of the early colonies . . . to stimulate and promote in any manner an interest in and a desire to preserve the principles of our early settlers and the standards which have made this country great."

Mr. and Mrs. Henry N. Flynt in Silver Shop
Exhibition Room

The trustees who have maintained these policies to date are:

Vincent Andrus†
Former Curator, American Wing,
Metropolitan Museum, New York, N.Y.

James Phinney Baxter III*
President Emeritus, Williams College,
Williamstown, Mass.

Frank L. Boyden
Headmaster, Deerfield Academy,
Deerfield, Mass.

Newton Brainard†
Former President,
Connecticut Historical Society,
Hartford, Conn.

Mrs. Francis B. Crowninshield†
Marblehead, Mass.

Henry F. DuPont‡
Wilmington, Del.

Mrs. Henry N. Flynt
Greenwich, Conn.

Henry N. Flynt, Jr.
Assistant Dean, Williams College,
Williamstown, Mass.

Henry N. Flynt
Greenwich, Conn.

Miss Elizabeth Fuller
Deerfield, Mass.

Frederick V. Geier
Chairman, Executive Committee,
Cincinnati Milling Machine Co.,
Cincinnati, Ohio

Wilmarth S. Lewis
Farmington, Conn., Editor, the Yale Edition of
Horace Walpole's Correspondence, and Senior
Fellow Emeritus, Yale University

John Mayer
Greenwich, Conn.

J. William Middendorf
Middendorf, Colgate Co.,
New York, N.Y.

Bruce McClellan
Headmaster, Lawrenceville School,
Lawrenceville, N.J.

Irving S. Olds†
Former Chairman, U.S. Steel Co., and President,
New York Historical Society, New York, N.Y.

Charles N. Stoddard, Jr.
Attorney, Greenfield, Mass.

Frederick Tomkins
Llewelyn Park, West Orange, N.J.

Alexander O. Vietor
Curator of Maps & Research Assistant,
Yale University, New Haven, Conn.

We are deeply indebted to J. Peter Spang III, Associate Curator, whose assistance, knowledge and taste have been of inestimable value to us and the organization. An educational program, designed to encourage male college undergraduates to enter the museum or American studies field as a life work, has completed its ninth year. Each year this course is gaining increased national significance. This and many new and thrilling phases of our educational, building, preservation and other projects are developing and will go forward, together with additions to the collections. We are heartened, inspired and stimulated by gifts for endowment and other purposes from friends and visitors. We appreciate that a broader base means a greater interest in the preservation movement generally, and a comprehensive understanding and appreciation of our efforts to the end that we may further the significant message of the historic past of our country.

* Retired.
† Deceased.
‡ Honorary.

Thus, through the united efforts of many individuals and groups, and the generosity of friends, the work goes forward, the programs continue, and still unfulfilled dreams may become a reality.

No one who visits Deerfield can fail to understand and enjoy the words of the local poet, David Morton, who wrote:

"The old names are here,
And the old forms
Not alone of doorways, of houses.
The light falls the way the light fell,
And it is not clear
In the elm shadows, if it be ourselves here,
Or others who were before us."

HELEN AND HENRY FLYNT
Deerfield, Massachusetts, 1965

INDEX

Dwight, Josiah, 149
Dwight, Timothy, 149
Dwight-Barnard House, 149-57; doctor's office in, 150; front doorway of, 166; kitchen of, 151; north chamber of, 156; parlor of, 153, 154, 171; south chamber of, 155

E

Eaglebrook School, 112
Earl, Ralph, 46, 48, 153
Edwards, Jonathan, 23
Eggleston, James, 6
Eliot, John, 4
Embroidery stand, in Ashley House, 33
Emerson, Ralph Waldo, 108

F

Faber, J., 24
Farrington House, 163
Field, David, 2, 15, 80
Fireplaces: in Allen House, 67, 70; in Ashley House, 25, 31; in Dwight-Barnard House, 151; in Frary House, 128, 129, 130, 131; in Hall Tavern, 101, 103, 105; in Old Indian House, 61; in Silver Shop, 58; in Wilson Printing House, 160
Flynt, Henry N., Jr., 173
Flynt, Mr. and Mrs. Henry N., 173, 174
Fogg, Bithia, portrait of, 33
Forster, Abraham, 84
Forster, Elinor, 56
Frary, John, 125
Frary, Nathan, 127
Frary, Samson, 5, 124
Frary House, 12, 15, 16, 117, 118, 124-32, 173; ballroom of, 131, 132; Blue Room of, 128; "borning room" of, 129; dining room of, 130; kitchen of, 129; parlor of, 128; south doorway of, 125; "summer kitchen" of, 130; upstairs chambers of, 132; see also Barnard Tavern
French attack on Deerfield, 9, 10
Frothingham, B., 170
Fuller, Elizabeth, 150, 174

G

Geier, Frederick V., 174
George III, portrait of, 30
Gere, Isaac, 57
Gibbs, Howard B., 112
Gillam, Charles, 74
Gillet, Joseph, 106
Greeley, Horace, 108

Greenfield, Mass., 16
Greenfield Gazette, 17
Greenleaf, Stephen, portrait of, 53
Greenwood, John, 82

H

Hadley, Mass., 5, 7
Hall, Joel, 95, 97
Hall, Lucretia, 95, 97
Hall Tavern, 95-105; ballroom of, 104, 105; bedroom of, 103; dining room of, 100, 104; doorway of, 167; family quarters of, 101; forge in, 99; parlor of, 102; workroom of, 101
Harrow (Hinsdale) House, 123, 168
Hawks, Eleazer, 163
Hawks, Molly Johnson, 51
Hawks, Susan, 44
Hawks, Zadock, 79
Heritage Foundation, 13, 58, 71, 91, 93, 150, 173
Higginson-Childs House, 157
Hildreth, Hosea, 108
Hildreth, Richard, 108
Hinsdale-Whiting House, 123, 168
Hinsdell, Ebenezer, 42
Hinsdell, Mehuman, 42
Hinsdell, Samuel, 5
Hinsdell House, 42, 43
Historical Society collections, 173
History of Deerfield, 44
Hitchcock family, 120
Hitchcock House, 120
Houghton, George H., 54
Housatonic Indians, 14
Howard, Thomas, 84
Hoyt, David, 60, 159
Hoyt, David Starr, 158
Hoyt, Epaphras, 120
Hoyt, Experience, 120
Hoyt, Mary, 152
Hoyt House, 158
Hoyt's Tavern, 15, 159
Hudley, Joseph, 13
Hurd, Nathaniel, 170

I

Indian House, Old, 11, 60-61, 139
Indian House Association, 173
Indians: as allies of French, 7, 8, 9, 10; Deerfield attacked by, 6-7, 9-10; prisoners killed by, 11; see also specific names of Indian tribes
Inkwell, brass, in Ashley House, 28